# DAILY GRAMS: Guided Review Aiding Mastery Skills

## GRADE 6

Author: Wanda C. Phillips

Published by ISHA Enterprises, Inc.
*Easy Grammar Systems™*
Post Office Box 25970
Scottsdale, Arizona  85255
**www.easygrammar.com**

## DAILY GRAMS:  GUIDED REVIEW AIDING MASTERY SKILLS – GRADE 6

# CAPITALIZATION
## Content and Sequence
## Grade 6

*Numbers indicate DAYS (page numbers) on which that concept is reviewed.*

**ABBREVIATION:**  5, 12, 14, 15, 17, 26, 55, 57, 61, 86, 105, 108, 152, 153, 157, 177

**AWARD:** 78

**BRAND NAME:**  91, 124

**BUSINESS:**  3, 18, 28, 32, 38, 40, 51, 53, 54, 77, 79, 87, 109, 120, 139, 149, 169, 178

**CLOSING of a LETTER:**  61, 84, 124, 139, 146

**CLUB/ORGANIZATION:**  29, 31, 45, 52, 63, 71, 80, 89, 125, 137, 172

**DAY of the WEEK:**  4, 53

**ETHNIC GROUP:**  65, 88, 133, 159

**FREEWAY/INTERSTATE/Etc.:**  34, 36, 87, 88, 111, 120, 150

**FRIENDLY LETTER:**  14, 23, 61, 84, 124, 139, 146

**GEOGRAPHIC PLACE:**

Basin:  150
Bay:  139
Beach:  2
Canyon:  127
Cave/Cavern:  179
Coast:  131
Continent:  9, 43, 47, 62, 95, 100, 154
Country:  13, 15, 44, 49, 62, 79, 100, 107, 113, 115, 132, 136, (142*), (145*), 154, 157, 158, 160, 167, 171, 174, 179
County:  162
Dam:  20
Desert:  11, 171
District:  15, 148
Forest (National):  72
Garden(s):  41
Glacier:  62
Gulf:  49, 68
Hemisphere:  112
Island(s):  96, 172
Lake:  20, 72
Mountain:  42, 81, 100, 114
Ocean:  95
Park:  38, 123, 137
Park (National):  64
Pass:  114, 140
Peninsula:  136
Recreational Area:  25
Region of Country:  18, (32*), 42, 48, 58, 60, 106, 110, (161*)
Region of World:  134, 169
Reservoir:  33
River:  135
Ruin(s):  135
Sea:  95
Site (Historic):  129
Spring(s):  81, 162
State:  4, 8, 10, 14, 20, 23, (32)*, 33, 41, 61, 81, 82, 84, 93, 97, 103, (114)*, 124, 127, 129, 131, 139, 143, 146, 150, 151, 153, 162
Territory:  24, 105, 113, 116
Township:  36

**TITLE in PLACE of a NAME:**   38, 40, 41, 53, 77, 91, 128, 162, 178

**TITLE of BOOKS and OTHER WORKS:**   7, 66, 74, 78, 83, 85, 93, 98, 103, 119, 121, 122, 130, 133, 144, 149, (157*), 176, 177

**TITLE of SHIP/PLANE/TRAIN:**   21, 44, 70, 136

**TITLE with a NAME** *(Captain, Mr., Aunt Tara, etc. )*:   1, 6, 21, 27, 28, 30, 40, 61, 65, 74, 75, 79, 86, 102, 105, 112, 116, 120, 121, 123, 126, 129, 134, 135, 141, 146, 151, 161, 168, 170, 173, 174, 176, 178

**DO NOT CAPITALIZE:**
   Animals:   11, 33, 42, 43, 73, 96, 106, 131, 154
   Career Choices:   26, 35, 54, 71, 102, 116, 145, 153, 167
   Directions:   3, 47, 51, 100, 143, 148, 171
   Diseases:   6, 30, 51, 56, 77, 97
   Foods:   32, 47, 53, 91
   Games:   30
   Musical Instruments:   66
   Plants:   28, 47, 137
   Seasons:   2, 94, 128
   School Subjects:   9, 22, 92, 126, 146

*Parentheses (   ) designate a relationship to another category.

# PUNCTUATION
## Content and Sequence
## Grade 6

*Numbers indicate DAYS (page numbers) on which that concept is reviewed.*

## APOSTROPHE:
Contraction:  1, 2, 3, 6, 10, 14, 17, 20, 21, 23, 25, 26, 38, 43, 44, 47, 62, 67, 70, 72, 75, 78, 83-85, 103, 119, 120, 123, 125, 127, 128, 134, 137, 141, 144, 149, 151, 153, 154, 160, 162, 164, 167, 168, 171, 172, 174, 176
Letter Out of Context + *s*:  124
OmittedLetter(s)/Number(s):  3, 49, 111, 168
Plural Possessive:  34, 35, 39, 57, 70, 73, 85, 107, 112, 121, 126, 140, 162, 169, 180
Singular Possessive:  12, 18, 20, 24, 29, 42, 58, 87, 94, 97, 104-106, 113, 123, 130, 136, 138, 144, 147, 149, 158, 160, 161, 172, 173

## COLON:
Greeting of a Business Letter:  66, 80, 93, 116, 132
List - Vertical and Within Sentence:  12, 23, 30, 84, 96, 108, 153
Time:  35, 73, 114, 122, 126, 152, 169

## COMMA:
Address Within Sentence (*I live at 1 Lu Lane, Reno, Nevada.*):  7, 16, 39, 57, 102, 148, 163, 179
Adjectives – Two Descriptive  (*long, cold winter*):  31, 44, 61, 70, 77, 79, 89, 100, 121, 125, 138, 142, 170, 177
Appositive:  8, 13, 46, 67, 68, 81, 100, 117, 118, 125, 129, 145, 147, 159, 166, 177
Clarity:  48
Closing of a Letter:  36, 56, 78, 94, 137, 146, 162
Company, Inc.:  66, 116, 132
Compound Sentence:  119, 146, 167, 176
Date (*January 1, 2000*):  4, 28, 51, 54, 56, 58, 60, 71, 78, 94, 101, 105, 137, 146
Date (*Monday, January 1*):  4, 35, 54, 71, 101, 122, 126
Date + Remainder of a Sentence:  54, 58, 71, 101, 105
Dependent Clause - Introductory:  47, 83, 103, 104, 120, 139, 141, 151, 154, 158, 162, 164, 168, 172, 179
Greeting of a Friendly letter:  36, 51, 56, 78, 94, 137, 146, 162
Interrupter:  10, 22, 31, 37, 62, 75, 111, 127, 131, 145, 149, 174, 176
Introductory Word(s):  3, 10, 46, 72, 145, 153, 171
Items in a Series:  2, 23, 30, 59, 72, 84, 96, 120, 121, 139, 141, 153, 159
Noun of Direct Address:  1, 6, 9, 14, 17, 33, 34, 37, 52, 70, 82, 83, 115, 124, 134, 153, 165, 171, 172, 175
Prepositional Phrase – Introductory:  105, 130
Quotation Marks:
    After Name of Person Speaking (*Tate said,*):  5, 17, 21, 38, 65, 98, 115, 134, 136, 150, 161, 165, 170, 175
    Within a Quotation (*"I like you," said Bob.*):  65, 97, 105, 107, 111, 115, 136, 144, 161, 170, 175, 180
Title After a Name (*Juan Lee,, M.D., is here.*):  43, 123, 142, 143
Town/City with Country (*Paris, France*):  114, 118, 137, 179
Town/City with State (*Ajo, AZ*):  11, 13, 14, 45, 49, 51, 54, 56, 60, 66, 78, 80, 81, 93-95, 100, 101, 110, 116, 123, 132, 137, 146, 152, 161, 162, 171
Town/City with State/Country + Sentence (*Ajo, Arizona, is lovely.*):  60, 94, 95, 114, 118, 137

## DASH:  95, 103, 150

## EXCLAMATION POINT:
Exclamatory Sentence:  29, 67, 86, 134, 160, 180
Interjection:  29, 67, 86, 134, 160

## HYPHEN:
Closely Related Words:  1, 22, 26, 28, 32, 37, 59, 62, 68, 74, 89, 94, 98, 121, 136, 142, 151, 161, 166, 170
Divided Word at End of Sentence:  82, 147
Fraction:  20, 24, 86, 140, 150, 155
Number:  18, 61, 97, 107, 110, 147, 166, 180

**PERIOD:**
   Abbreviation: 4, 9, 11-13, 19, 32-34, 42, 43, 45, 46, 53, 54, 56, 60, 63-66, 73, 78, 80, 82, 92, 93, 98, 116-118, 123, 126, 132, 136, 137, 142, 143, 146, 153, 157, 161-163, 171, 173, 180
   Outline: 41, 91
   Sentence ending: 2-8, 10-13, 16-18, 20-26, 28, 30-32, 35-39, 43, 44, 46-49, 52, 54, 57-62, 65, 67, 68, 70-73, 75, 77-79, 81, 83, 85, 87, 89, 94, 96-98, 100-107, 111, 113, 114, 117-131, 136-149, 151-155, 158, 159, 161-164, 166-174, 176, 177, 179, 180

**PARENTHESES:** 95, 103, 150

**PUNCTUATION Used in a Friendly Letter:** 36, 56, 162

**QUESTON MARK:** 1, 9, 14, 33, 34, 42, 74, 82, 84, 94, 110, 112, 115, 150, 165, 175

**QUOTATION MARKS:**
   Direct Quotations:
      Occurring at Beginning *("Go!" said Toni.)*: 97, 105, 107, 111, 144, 160
      Occurring at End *(Toni yelled, "Go!")*: 5, 17, 21, 38, 98, 134, 150, 165
      Split: 65, 115, 136, 161, 170, 175, 180
   Titles:
      Article: 40, 50, 69, 76, 82, 99, 129, 133, 156, 178
      Chapter: 55, 133
      Essay: 27, 104, 109, 173
      Nursery Rhyme: 88, 178
      Poem: 27, 69, 99, 106, 135, 138, 178
      Song: 32, 55, 88, 112, 113, 135, 178
      Story: 15, 76, 88, 109, 130, 178

**SEMICOLON:** 85, 127, 128, 149, 174

**UNDERLINING:**
   Letter(s)/Number(s)/Word(s) Out of Context: 52, 124, 154, 165
   Name of Ship/Plane/Train: 67, 69, 87, 114, 122, 152, 169, 171, 179
   Titles:
      Album/Compact Disk (CD): 88, 135, 178
      Book: 15, 27, 40, 50, 69, 109, 135, 155, 164, 178
      Magazine: 40, 50, 55, 69, 76, 77, 133, 156, 178
      Movie/Video: 25, 50, 74, 144, 156
      Newspaper: 55, 99, 109, 178
      Play: 76, 88, 133, 178
      Television Show: 79, 88, 115, 156
      Work of Art: 99

Note: Concepts may be included under other headings as well. For example, interjections will also be reviewed within the "Grammar and Other Concepts" division. However, those have not been listed within this scope and sequence.

# GRAMMAR AND OTHER CONCEPTS
## Content and Sequence
## Grade 6

*Numbers indicate DAYS (page numbers) on which that concept is reviewed.*

## ADJECTIVES:
Adjective or Adverb:  10, 34, 53, 73, 79, 104, 143, 162, 172, 177, 179
Adjective or Noun:  66, 86, 99, 128, 169
Adjective or Pronoun:  92
Degrees:  27, 48, 83, 107, 167
Descriptive:  1, 11, 60, 80, 102, 145, 156, 157, 180
Identification of All Adjectives:  102, 156, 180
Limiting:  13, 30, 38, 52, 90, 92, 102, 154, 156, 180
Predicate Adjectives:  91, 118
Proper Adjectives:  18, 45, 68

## ADVERBS:
Adverb or Adjective:  10, 34, 53, 73, 79, 104, 143, 162, 172, 177, 179
Adverb or Preposition:  95, 123, 145, 165
Degrees:  26, 47, 66, 94, 106, 131, 175
Double Negatives:  24, 76, 111, 125, 137, 159
How:  11, 17, 32, 65, 121, 157
To What Extent:  21, 41, 63, 101, 134, 156
Use of Well:  53, 73, 94, 104, 121, 162, 172, 179
When:  14, 44, 49, 101, 121, 156
Where:  14, 17, 36, 49, 59, 101

## ANALOGIES:  1, 8, 11, 13, 14, 19, 22, 23, 25, 31, 33, 38, 40-42, 47, 50, 53, 55, 56, 60, 61, 70, 72, 77, 79, 82, 84, 86, 88, 92, 93, 95, 97, 101, 103, 108, 110, 113, 115, 118, 121, 122, 124, 126, 130, 132, 133, 138, 140, 142, 144, 147, 150, 152, 155, 156, 157, 162, 163, 165, 166, 169, 171, 172, 175, 177, 178, 180

## CATEGORIES:  36, 37

## CLAUSES (Dependent/Independent):  45, 63, 68, 73, 75, 81, 83, 91, 99, 100, 102, 107, 132, 134

## CONJUNCTIONS:
Coordinating:  7, 12, 46, 69, 88, 132, 178
Correlative:  161

## DICTIONARY SKILLS:
Alphabetizing:  16, 37, 56, 69, 81, 99, 105, 126, 138, 150
Guide Words:  23, 49, 84, 122, 159, 178

## DIFFICULT WORDS:
Affect/Effect:  124, 149
Can/May:  133, 153, 162
It's/Its:  19, 73, 112, 114, 179
They're/Their/There:  6, 19, 52, 73, 93, 112, 114, 124, 149, 179
To/Two/Too:  6, 52, 114
You're/Your:  6, 19, 52, 73, 93, 112, 133, 144, 179
We're/Were:  73

## FRIENDLY LETTERS
Envelopes:  113, 117, 126, 149, 152
Letter Parts:  22, 46, 72, 139, 146, 162

## INTERJECTIONS:  8, 42, 68, 85, 130

**SYNONYMS/ANTONYMS/HOMONYMS:**  2, 9, 12, 17, 30, 50, 62, 87, 103, 125, 141, 147, 174

**VERBS:**
  Action or Linking:  91, 151, 170
  Can/May:  133, 153, 162
  Compound:  40, 64, 109, 124, 136, 171
  Contraction:  1, 26, 43, 67, 77, 100, 148
  Helping Verb(s)/Verb Phrase:  3, 5, 21, 60, 72, 80, 101, 120, 166, 180
  Infinitive:  92, 113, 135, 169
  Linking:  137, 151
  Past Participle Construction of Irregular Verbs:  5, 21, 60, 101, 128, 133, 135, 153, 158, 180
  Present Participle Construction:  116, 128
  Regular/Irregular:  31, 55, 82, 167
  Sit/Set, Lie/Lay, Rise/Raise:  5, 72, 180
  Subject/Verb Agreement:  4, 33, 57, 58, 67, 75, 103, 112, 127, 160, 177
  Subject/Verb Identification:  3, 7, 9, 17, 20, 25, 27, 40, 44, 48, 54, 58, 62, 64, 74, 78, 82, 83, 95, 104, 105, 109, 124, 127, 129, 136, 139, 164, 171
  Tenses:
    Present/Past/Future:  12, 15, 35, 38, 61, 74, 110, 130, 144, 154, 155, 158, 168
    Perfect Tense:  95, 103, 130, 168

*Parentheses ( ) designate a relationship to another category, also.

The purpose of <u>**DAILY GRAMS:  GUIDED REVIEW AIDING MASTERY**</u> <u>**SKILLS – GRADE 6**</u> is to provide students with daily review of their language. Review of concepts helps to promote **mastery learning**.

All *Daily Grams* are review texts.  If you are familiar with grades three, four, and five, you are aware that those books contain a great deal of built-in instruction along with the review.  Less instruction is included within this text.  As in all *Daily Grams*, concepts are usually repeated within twenty-five to thirty days.  Like *Daily Grams – Grade 5*, this text has six items per page and includes instruction and built-in review of analogies, spelling, and simple/compound/complex sentences.

## FORMAT

Each page is set up in this manner:

1.  Sentence # 1 is always **capitalization** review.

2.  Sentence #2 is always **punctuation** review.  Students will insert needed punctuation.  You may, however, want students to write this sentence, adding needed punctuation.

3.  Numbers 3 and 4 address **general concepts**.  You may wish to replace one of these items with material you are currently studying, especially if the concept provided has not yet been introduced.

4.  In number 5, **spelling** rules, **analogies**, and **simple/compound/complex sentences** are introduced and reviewed.

5.  Number 6 is always **sentence combining**.  Using the sentences given, students will write one higher-level sentence.  If you feel that the sentences provided are too difficult, simply delete parts or replace them.  If you feel that a particular combining is too easy, add more detail and/or information.

<u>**DAILY GRAMS: GUIDED REVIEW AIDING MASTERY SKILLS – GRADE 6**</u> is designed as a guided review. There are **180 lessons** in this book, one review per teaching day. *DAILY GRAMS* will take approximately **10 minutes** total time; this includes both completing and grading. (Do not be concerned if this takes slightly longer.)

## <u>PROCEDURE</u>

1.  Students should do "GRAMS" immediately upon entering the classroom or beginning the language class. Each lesson should be copied for each student, written on the board, or placed on a transparency for use with an overhead projector. (The projector may need to be adjusted to enlarge the print.)

2.  Students will finish at different rates. Two ideas are suggested:

    A.  Students may read when finished.

    B.  Students may write in daily journals.

    Obviously, you know your students well and will adjust these to align with your students' needs and your own expectations.

3.  Discuss answers orally as a class. (Examples: Why is *Italian* capitalized? Why do we insert a comma after the person's name in this sentence?)

4.  In making students accountable for this type of activity, you may want to Take an occasional quiz grade.

# SUGGESTIONS

1. Make transparencies and file them. These can be used each year. Simply draw that day's "GRAMS" from your file.

   You may choose to purchase a **workbook** for each student or to make copies for each student. A transparency is still needed. Students usually learn more by seeing the answers.

2. Allow students to use a dictionary, if necessary, to complete analogies.

3. Solicit as much student response as possible. Keep the lessons lively!

4. If possible, allow students to write sentence combinings on the board. Use these for class "editing" and **praise**!

5. As one progresses through this book, some of the sentence combinings become longer and more complex. This may necessitate an adaptation to your own teaching style and to your students' needs.

   *Note:* **Workbooks** include all of the daily reviews contained within the teacher text. They do not include the introductory pages or the answers.

**CAPITALIZATION:**

1.  tony and i like to speak spanish with uncle marco.

**PUNCTUATION:**

2.  Tina wheres your six speed bike

**PARTS OF SPEECH:**

   **Circle any descriptive adjectives:**

3.  A fierce tropical storm is coming.

**PARTS OF SPEECH:    VERBS**

   **Write the contraction:**

4.  A.  have not - _____         D.  I shall - _____

   B.  they are - _____          E.  do not - _____

   C.  is not - _____            F.  you are - _____

**ANALOGIES:**

**Analogies show relationships.**  First, determine how the first two words (set) of an analogy are related (alike, opposite, part of a whole, etc.).  After determining the relationship of the first two words, look at the third word and the answers.  The third word and your answer (second set) must show the same relationship.
   **Synonyms may be expressed in the relationship.**
      Find is to discover as dig is to _____.
      (a) recover    (b) demote    (c) hoist    **(d) excavate**
   Analogies are usually presented in an equation.  Read it exactly as above.
      Find : discover :: dig : _____
      (a) recover    (b) demote    (c) hoist    **(d) excavate**

   **Circle the answer that best completes the analogy:**

5.  give : donate :: imagine : _____
    (a) mind       (b) visualize     (c) react      (d) demonstrate

**SENTENCE COMBINING:**

6.  These brownies are chocolate.
    They have marshmallow on the inside.

    _____

    _____

**DAY 2**

**CAPITALIZATION:**

1.   during their winter break, they went to ke'e beach.

**PUNCTUATION:**

2.   Theyll swim play games and eat hot dogs at the party

**PARTS OF SPEECH:**

Cross out the prepositional phrase and label the object of the preposition – <u>O.P.</u>:

3.   Beans were planted in the garden.

**PARTS OF SPEECH:**

4.   An example of a concrete noun is _____.

**SYNONYMS/ANTONYMS:**

Synonyms are words that have similar meanings.
Antonyms are words with opposite meanings.

Write <u>Syn.</u> if the words are synonyms; write <u>Ant.</u> if the words are antonyms:

5.   A.  _____   legal – lawful          C.  _____   forgive – pardon
     B.  _____   unsure – certain        D.  _____   important – relevant

**SENTENCE COMBINING:**

6.   The first trolleys were drawn by horses.
     The first buses were drawn by horses.

     _____

     _____

**CAPITALIZATION:**

1.   the carr family traveled west on greenbriar road to wooley department store.

**PUNCTUATION:**

2.   No I wont be there by 2 oclock

**SENTENCE TYPES:**

   **Determine the type of sentence:**

3.  A.   This jello has melted.                         _____

    B.   Have the baby birds left their nest?       _____

**SUBJECT/VERB:**
   **Cross out any prepositional phrases.  Underline the subject once and the verb or verb phrase twice:**
        **Remember:   helping verb  +  main verb  =  verb phrase**
              Example:   should have  +  gone  =  should have gone

4.   During the game, her parents had cheered loudly.

**ANALOGIES:**

   **Circle the answer that best completes the analogy:**

5.   forgive : pardon :: declare : _____
       (a) predict       (b) diminish       (c) state       (d) inquire

**SENTENCE COMBINING:**

6.   The baby blanket is white.
     It has duck designs.

     _____

     _____

## DAY 4

**CAPITALIZATION:**

1. "we will spend the last sunday in march with our friends from kansas," said jemima.

**PUNCTUATION:**

2. The bus left on Thurs May 9 2001

**PARTS OF SPEECH:   NOUNS**

**Write the possessive:**

3. A.  a toy belonging to a child = a _____ toy

   B.  a puppy belonging to two girls = the _____ puppy

**PARTS OF SPEECH:   VERBS**

**Circle the correct verb:**

4. Our dad ( run, runs ) a mile every day.

**SPELLING:**
**Words ending in consonant + e usually drop the e when adding a suffix (ending) beginning with a vowel.  They usually do not drop the e when adding a suffix starting with a consonant.**
Examples:   retire + ed = retired        retire + ment = retirement

**Write the correct spelling of the following words:**

5. A.  note + ed - _____

   B.  locate + or - _____

   C.  taste + less - _____

**SENTENCE COMBINING:**

6. Their nephew plays on a hockey team.
   He is a goalie.

   _____

   _____

**CAPITALIZATION:**

1.  they toured the crime lab of the f. b. i. building which is near the white house.

**PUNCTUATION:**

2.  Linda said  Were eating soon

**PARTS OF SPEECH:   PRONOUNS**
    **Circle the correct answer:**

3.  ( Me and Tom ) ( Tom and I ) talked to his parents.

**PARTS OF SPEECH:   VERBS**

   **Underline the verb phrase twice:**

4.  A.  They have ( rode, ridden ) horses often.

    B.  This entry wasn't ( chose, chosen ) as the winner.

    C.  The book has ( laid, lain ) on the table for a week.

    D.  David had ( brought, brung ) his brother along.

**SPELLING:**

   **Write the correct spelling of the following words:**

5.  A.  dare + ing - _____

    B.  debate + or - _____

    C.  lone + some - _____

**SENTENCE COMBINING:**

6.  Professor Stein went to Iona.
    Iona is an island.
    It is part of Scotland.

    _____

    _____

## DAY 6

**CAPITALIZATION:**

1.    has mr. davis gone to st. mary's hospital for diabetes testing?

**PUNCTUATION:**

2.    Lets go to the park Andy

**PARTS OF SPEECH:    NOUNS**

Write <u>C</u> if the noun is common and <u>P</u> if the noun is proper:

3.    A.  \_\_\_\_  bird                    D.  \_\_\_\_  Lake Superior

       B.  \_\_\_\_  hummingbird       E.  \_\_\_\_  Seattle

       C.  \_\_\_\_  Mary                  F.  \_\_\_\_  lake

**DIFFICULT WORDS:**
   Circle the correct answer:

4.    A.    ( There, Their, They're ) friends helped with the chores.
       B.    ( To, Too, Two ) trees had fallen during the storm.
       C.    ( Your, You're ) a great skater.

**PHRASES/CLAUSES:**
   A phrase is a group of words; it doesn't contain a subject and a verb.
                   Examples:   behind the chair                speaking slowly

   A clause contains a subject and a verb.    Example:   Her <u>hair</u> <u>is</u> red.

   Write <u>P</u> if the group of words is a phrase; write <u>C</u> if the group of words is a clause:

5.    A.   \_\_\_\_   Reviewing for a test.
       B.   \_\_\_\_   He is very witty.

**SENTENCE COMBINING:**

6.    The hand has twenty-seven bones.
       They are small.
       They are moved by thirty-seven muscles.

_____

_____

**CAPITALIZATION:**
   **Capitalize these titles:**

1. A. "home on the range"

   B. "love and a question"


**PUNCTUATION:**

2. His new address is 127 Low Dutch Road Gettysburg PA   17325


**SUBJECT/VERB:**

**Cross out any prepositional phrases.  Underline the subject once and the verb or verb phrase twice:**
**Remember:   helping verb  +  main verb  =  verb phrase**
Example:   might have  +  looked  =  might have looked

3. I must have taken a wrong turn.


**PARTS OF SPEECH:    CONJUNCTIONS**

**Write a conjunction in the space provided:**

4. Mrs. Johnson _____ Mr. Haines will lead the discussion.


**PHRASES/CLAUSES:**

**Write P if the group of words is a phrase; write C if the group of words is a clause:**
**Remember:   A clause contains a subject and a verb.**

5. A. _____ With a startled look.

   B. _____ Ten millimeters equal a centimeter.


**SENTENCE COMBINING:**

6. That girl is selling cookies for a fund raiser.
   She attends my school.

   _____

   _____

**DAY 8**

**CAPITALIZATION:**

1.   does jacy live on east bellview avenue in newport, rhode island?

**PUNCTUATION:**

2.   Barbara my cousin is a gymnast

**PARTS OF SPEECH:   INTERJECTIONS**

**Interjections are words or phrases that show emotion.**

3.   Write an example of an interjection:  _____

**PARTS OF SPEECH:   NOUNS**

**Write the plural:**

4.   A.  rug - _____       D.  house - _____

     B.  flash - _____       E.  bay - _____

     C.  mouse - _____       F.  story - _____

**ANALOGIES:**

**Circle the answer that best completes the analogy:**

5.   buyer : purchaser :: busybody : _____
     (a) guard       (b) supporter       (c) worker       (d) meddler

**SENTENCE COMBINING:**

6.   Lani is riding her exercise bike.
     Lani is also reading.

     _____

     _____

**CAPITALIZATION:**

1.   he made a map of south america in his geography class at freet middle school.

**PUNCTUATION:**

2.   Did you Mrs Benson find my notebook or language book

**PARTS OF SPEECH:    PREPOSITIONS**
   **Cross out any prepositional phrases.  Underline the subject once and the verb or verb phrase twice:**

3.   The lady with the poodle is very funny.

**ANTONYMS/HOMONYMS/SYNONYMS:**
   **Antonyms are words with opposite meanings.**
   **Synonyms are words with similar meanings.**
   **Homonyms are words that sound alike but are spelled differently.**

4.   A.   A synonym for *wait* is _____.

     B.   A homonym for *wait* is _____.

     C.   An antonym for *wait* is _____.

**SPELLING:**

   **Words ending with vowel + vowel + consonant  (VVC) usually just add a suffix.**

      Example:   meet + ing = meet**ing**         rejoin + ed = rejoin**ed**

   **Write the correct spelling of the following words:**

5.   A.   steam + ing - _____

     B.   strain + ed - _____

     C.   redeem + er - _____

**SENTENCE COMBINING:**

6.   Clotted cream is chiefly made in England.
     It is also called Devonshire cream.

     _____

     _____

**DAY 10**

**CAPITALIZATION:**

1.  brad and i attended main street mayfest in roxboro, north carolina, last year.

**PUNCTUATION:**

2.  Yes in fact youre correct about that

**PARTS OF SPEECH:   ADVERBS/ADJECTIVES**

 **Circle the correct word:**

3.  Jodi cleans her room ( good, well ).

**SENTENCE TYPES:**

 **Determine the type of sentence:**

4.  A.  Please put this away. _____
    B.  Our team won! _____

**PHRASES/CLAUSES:**

 **Write P if the group of words is a phrase; write C if the group of words is a clause:**
  **Remember:   A clause contains a subject and a verb.**

5.  A.  _____  Intending to stay up late
    B.  _____  When they go to the movies

**SENTENCE COMBINING:**

6.  Stella bought a horse.
    It is an Arabian.
    She bought it in Santa Fe.
    She bought it last week.

    _____

    _____

**CAPITALIZATION:**

1. candace said, "a piebald chuckwalla lives in the mojave desert."

**PUNCTUATION:**

2. Miss Mary E Ortiz works for Bart Co in Tulsa Oklahoma

**PARTS OF SPEECH:    ADJECTIVES**

   **Circle any descriptive adjectives:**

3. The bride wore a white embroidered gown.

**PARTS OF SPEECH:    ADVERBS**

   **Circle any adverbs that tell *how*:**

4. Polly brushed her teeth slowly and thoroughly.

**ANALOGIES:**

   **Antonyms or words with opposite meanings may be expressed in a relationship.**
     Busy : idle :: normal : _____
     (a)  usual    (b)  frequent    **(c)  bizarre**    (d)  routine

   **Circle the answer that best completes the analogy:**

5. flabby : toned :: pleased : _____
     (a) offended        (b) delighted        (c) stunned        (d) optional

**SENTENCE COMBINING:**

6. The cupboard is pine.
   The cupboard has glass doors.
   We bought the cupboard at an auction.

   _____

   _____

**DAY 12**

**CAPITALIZATION:**

1. the persian empire existed from 538-333 b. c.

**PUNCTUATION:**

2. Nancys guest list includes the following  Mr L Sing  Dr Lin Wong and Mrs Chika Cole

**PARTS OF SPEECH:     VERBS**

    **Write the verb tenses:**

3.   A. _____   Dena **likes** sherbet.

     B. _____   They **will go** to a lake.

     C. _____   He **took** off his hat.

**PARTS OF SPEECH:     CONJUNCTIONS**

4. The three common coordinating conjunctions are _____, _____, and _____.

**SYNONYMS/ANTONYMS:**

    **Synonyms are words that have similar meanings.**
    **Antonyms are words with opposite meanings.**

    **Write <u>Syn</u>. if the words are synonyms; write <u>Ant</u>. if the words are antonyms:**

5.   A. _____   admit – deny      C. _____   hate – detest
     B. _____   quit – resign      D. _____   veto – approve

**SENTENCE COMBINING:**

6. A toad has a forked tongue.
    A toad has a sticky tongue.
    A toad uses its tongue to capture insects.

_____

_____

**CAPITALIZATION:**

1. a frenchman named lafayette helped america during the revolutionary war.

**PUNCTUATION:**

2. Rev R C Collins my minister was born in Lake Wales Florida

**PARTS OF SPEECH:    ADJECTIVES**

3. The articles that are really a type of adjective are _____, _____, and _____.

**PREFIXES/ROOT WORDS/SUFFIXES:**

The prefix <u>sub</u> means *under*.  The root word <u>terra</u> means *earth*.

4. Where is a subterranean passage? _____

_____

**ANALOGIES:**

Antonyms may be expressed in analogies.

Circle the answer that best completes the analogy:

5. dull : glowing :: stingy : _____
   (a) mean      (b) miserly      (c) selfish      (d) generous

**SENTENCE COMBINING:**

6. The ear is the organ of hearing.
   The ear is also the organ of balance.

_____

_____

**DAY 14**

**CAPITALIZATION:**

1.                                                                       12337 clemmens lane
                                                                          fallbrook, ca  92028
                                                                          july 25, 2012


      dear anne,


**PUNCTUATION:**

2.   Nikko werent you born in Honolulu Hawaii


**PARTS OF SPEECH:    ADVERBS**

   **Circle any adverbs telling *where* or *when*:**

3.   Would you like to sit here now and move to the front row later?


**PARTS OF SPEECH:    PRONOUNS**

   **Circle the correct pronoun:**

4.   She doesn't want to go with ( they, them ).


**ANALOGIES:**

   **Circle the answer that best completes the analogy:**

5.   tall : short :: accidental : _____
      (a) accident     (b) unimportant     (c) deliberate     (d) careless


**SENTENCE COMBINING:**

6.   Kurt read the back of the cereal box.
      Kurt put the cereal box into his cart.

      _____

      _____

**CAPITALIZATION:**

1.   the u. s. capitol in washington, d. c., is close to union station.

**PUNCTUATION:**

   **Punctuate these titles:**

2.   A.   (book)      The Black Stallion
      B.   (story)      Sunday for Sona


**PARTS OF SPEECH:**
   **Write the present tense of each infinitive:**

3.   A.   to yell - _____

      B.   to break - _____


**PARTS OF SPEECH:   PRONOUNS**
   **Circle the correct pronoun:**

4.   His father and ( he, him ) will hike tomorrow.


**SPELLING:**

   **Write the correct spelling of the following words:**

5.   A.   lose + ing - _____

      B.   shame + ful - _____

      C.   sure + ly - _____


**SENTENCE COMBINING:**

6.   Danno is wearing a suit.
      The suit is pinstriped.
      Danno is wearing the suit for an interview.

   _____

   _____

# DAY 16

## CAPITALIZATION:

**Capitalize this outline:**

1.   i.   arizona cities

        a.   population under a million

        b.   population over a million

## PUNCTUATION:

2.   Their address is 4 Fordham Road Tulsa Oklahoma   74033

## PARTS OF SPEECH:   PREPOSITIONS

**Circle any prepositions in the following sentence:**

3.   During the storm in August, one of our trees tumbled to the ground.

## DICTIONARY:   ALPHABETIZING

**Place the following words in alphabetical order:**

4.   forest     hamlet     fruit     garage     dessert

    (a) _____     (c) _____     (e) _____

    (b) _____     (d) _____

## SPELLING:

**Write the correct spelling of the following words:**

5.   A.   manage + er - _____

    B.   manage + ing - _____

    C.   manage + ment - _____

## SENTENCE COMBINING:

6.   Kalingrad is a seaport.
     It is located on the Baltic Sea.
     It is ice-free.

_____

_____

**CAPITALIZATION:**

1.  in 330 a. d., constantinople became the capital of the roman empire.

**PUNCTUATION:**

2.  The leader said  Thats a good idea Sam

**PARTS OF SPEECH:**

   **Circle any adverbs that tell *how* or *where*:**

3.  May we sit there together?

**SUBJECT/VERB:**

   **Place one line under the subject and two lines under the verb or verb phrase:**

   **Remember:   helping verb(s)   +   main verb   =   verb phrase**

   Example:   will be   +   going   =   will be going

4.  Several trucks were already loaded.

**SYNONYMS/ANTONYMS:**

   **Synonyms are words that have similar meanings.**
   **Antonyms are words with opposite meanings.**

   **Write <u>Syn</u>. if the words are synonyms; write <u>Ant</u>. if the words are antonyms:**

5.  A. _____   worried – carefree          C. _____   cashier – clerk
    B. _____   rigid – inflexible           D. _____   dilute – concentrate

**SENTENCE COMBINING:**

6.  Tara is sanding a log.
    Tara is making a bed.
    The bed is for her niece.

    _____

    _____

**DAY 18**

**CAPITALIZATION:**

1.  their family rode the blue ridge scenic railway during their trip to the south.


**PUNCTUATION:**

2.  Jacobs grandparents have given him twenty one books


**PARTS OF SPEECH:    NOUNS**

 Nouns name persons, places, things, and ideas.

  Circle any nouns in the following sentence:

3.  A tall oak tree is in the backyard of their house.


**PARTS OF SPEECH:    ADJECTIVES**

  Write the proper adjective derived from a proper noun:

4.  A.  France - _____     C.  China - _____

    B.  Switzerland - _____     D.  America - _____


**SPELLING:**

**Remember:**   Words ending in vowel + consonant + e usually drop the e when adding a suffix beginning with a vowel.

  Write the correct spelling of the following words:

5.  A.  declare + ing - _____     C.  announce + ment - _____

    B.  spite + ful - _____     D.  precise + ly - _____


**SENTENCE COMBINING:**

6.  An armored car stopped in front of a jewelry store.
    The driver entered the jewelry store.

    _____

    _____

**CAPITALIZATION:**
**Capitalize these lines of poetry from the poem, "Steam Shovel," by Charles Mann.**

1.  the dinosaurs are not all dead.

    i saw one raise its iron head

    to watch me walking down the road

    beyond our house today.

**PUNCTUATION:**

**Write the abbreviation:**

2.  A.  United States - _____       C.  inch - _____

    B.  building - _____       D.  Senator - _____

**PARTS OF SPEECH:     PREPOSITIONS**
**Circle any object(s) of the preposition in the following sentence:**

3.  In July my brother went to a camp with his church group.

**DIFFICULT WORDS:**
**Circle the correct answer:**

4.  A.  Let's go if ( there, their, they're ) ready.

    B.  A lion lifted ( its, it's ) head and sniffed.

    C.  ( Your, You're ) button is dangling from your shirt.

**ANALOGIES:**
**Circle the answer that best completes the analogy:**

5.  wild : tame :: fake : _____
    (a) false       (b) counterfeit       (c) money       (d) genuine

**SENTENCE COMBINING:**

6.  The kitchen chair needs to be repaired.
    The back has fallen off.

    _____

    _____

**DAY 20**

**CAPITALIZATION:**

1.  the visitors saw garrison dam which is on lake sakokawea in north dakota.

**PUNCTUATION:**

2.  Three fourths of Raymonds baseball cards arent new

**SUBJECT/VERB:**

**A compound subject refers to more than one.**

**Underline the subject once and the verb or verb phrase twice:**

3.  John and Holly mowed the grass.

**PARTS OF SPEECH:**

**Write the possessive form:**

4.  A.  a hamster belonging to my sister - _____

    B.  a hamster belonging to three sisters - _____

**SPELLING:**

**Words that end in a vowel plus two or more consonants usually just add a suffix.**

Example:   respond + ed = responded

**Write the correct spelling of the following words:**

5.  A.  return + able - _____

    B.  ghost + ly - _____

    C.  thought + ful - _____

**SENTENCE COMBINING:**

6.  Her first name was not spelled correctly.
    Her last name was also misspelled.

    _____

    _____

**CAPITALIZATION:**

1. did captain christopher jones bring the pilgrims on the ship, <u>mayflower</u>?


**PUNCTUATION:**

2. David said  I cant go


**PARTS OF SPEECH:**
   **Unscramble these adverbs that tell *to what extent:***

3. A. tno - _____          D. ahtrer - _____          G. os - _____

   B. oto - _____          E. eqtiu - _____

   C. vyre - _____         F. hwtsoame - _____


**PARTS OF SPEECH:   VERBS**

   **Underline the verb phrase twice:**

4. A. I could have ( swam, swum ) more laps.

   B. Has anyone ( saw, seen ) my coat?

   C. Jack must have ( drawn, drew ) that picture.

   D. That record was ( broke, broken ) recently.


**SPELLING:**

   **Write the correct spelling of the following words:**

5. A. locate + or - _____

   B. bloat + ed - _____

   C. use + ful - _____


**SENTENCE COMBINING:**

6. Siamese cats have almond-shaped eyes.
   Their eyes are blue.

   _____

   _____

**DAY 22**

**CAPITALIZATION:**

1.  alex asked, "did you study judaism in your world religion class?"

**PUNCTUATION:**

2.  This steak I think is well done

**PARTS OF SPEECH:    NOUNS**

   **Write C if the noun is concrete; write A if the noun is abstract:**

3.  A.  ____  peace          C.  ____  street

    B.  ____  sunglasses     D.  ____  kindness

**FRIENDLY LETTER:**
   **Label the parts of this friendly letter: (A) heading   (B) closing   (C) greeting
   (D) signature   (E) body**

4.                          ( )       11 Coral Avenue
                                      Duluth, MN  55820
                                      April 23, 20—
      ( )       Dear Patti,
      ( )           We want to let you know we will be coming in July.
                Our family plans to leave here after Independence Day!
                             ( )          Your cousin,
                             ( )          Carlos

**ANALOGIES:**

   **Circle the answer that best completes the analogy:**

5.  marry : wed :: subtract : _____
    (a) add      (b) deduct      (c) math      (d) return

**SENTENCE COMBINING:**

6.  Tanning leather makes it stronger.
    It also makes it more flexible.

    _____

    _____

**CAPITALIZATION:**

1.                                               5470 east monroe street
                                                marathon, new york   13803
                                                january 15, 20—


     dear frank and anna,


**PUNCTUATION:**

2.   Theyre planning on ordering the following   coke pizza and yogurt


**PARTS OF SPEECH:   PREPOSITIONS**

   **Cross out any prepositional phrases; circle any object of the preposition:**

3.   The sweater from my aunt is too small.


**LIBRARY SKILLS:**

4.   The three types of cards in the card catalog are _____, _____,

     and _____.


**ANALOGIES:**

   **Circle the answer that best completes the analogy:**

5.   conflict : peace :: excitement : _____
     (a) fun      (b) boredom      (c) appreciation      (d) attendance


**SENTENCE COMBINING:**

6.   Cricket is a ball game.
     It is played by two teams.
     Flat bats are used.

     _____

     _____

## DAY 24

### CAPITALIZATION:

1.  joe juneau died in the yukon territory but was buried in evergreen cemetery in the town he had founded.

### PUNCTUATION:

2.  Two fifths of Brads family should be arriving soon

### DICTIONARY:    GUIDE WORDS

**Guide Words            mint          mutt**

**Will the following words be found on a dictionary page with the guide words, *mint* and *mutt*?  Write <u>Yes</u> or <u>No</u> in the blank:**

3.  A. _____ mother          C. _____ matter

    B. _____ meant           D. _____ music

### PARTS OF SPEECH:    ADVERBS
**Circle the correct word:**

4.  The librarian hasn't given the book to ( anybody, nobody ).

### SPELLING:
**Write the correct spelling of the following words:**

5.  A.  crusade + ing - _____

    B.  blame + less - _____

    C.  depend + able - _____

### SENTENCE COMBINING:

6.  Faith rubbed her eyes.
    Faith was sleepy.

    _____

    _____

**CAPITALIZATION:**

1.  have molly and he ever biked in cuyahoga valley national recreation area?


**PUNCTUATION:**

2.  Were seeing the movie entitled David and Goliath today


**SUBJECT/VERB:**

**Cross out any prepositional phrases.  Underline the subject once and the verb or verb phrase twice:**

3.  One of the raccoons waded across the street.


**LIBRARY SKILLS:**

4.  Books that are true are called _____.


**ANALOGIES:**

**Circle the answer that best completes the analogy:**

5.  cheerfully : joyfully :: fondly : _____
    (a) affectionately     (b) clearly     (c) blustery     (d) artfully


**SENTENCE COMBINING:**

6.  Jamaica is an island of the West Indies.
    It is located south of Florida.

    _____

    _____

**DAY 26**

**CAPITALIZATION:**

1.   william l. shoemaker, a successful jockey, won four kentucky derbies.


**PUNCTUATION:**

2.   Youre usually happy go lucky and carefree


**PARTS OF SPEECH:    VERBS**

   **Write the contraction:**

3.   A.   do not - _____        D.   cannot - _____

      B.   I am - _____         E.   they have - _____

      C.   we are - _____       F.   they will - _____


**PARTS OF SPEECH:    ADVERBS**
   **Circle the correct adverb:**

4.   Rob hit the ball ( harder, hardest ) than his cousin.


**PHRASES/CLAUSES:**

   **A phrase is a group of words.**
          Examples:    after dinner
                       running in the rain

   **A clause contains a subject and verb/verb phrase.**
          Examples:    This <u>candy sizzles</u> in your mouth.
                       When <u>you have driven</u> this car

   **Write <u>P</u> if the group of words is a phrase; write <u>C</u> if the group of words is a clause:**

5.   A.   _____        down the street

      B.   _____        The jury presented the verdict.


**SENTENCE COMBINING:**

6.   Bertie likes to perch on my finger.
     Bertie is my sister's parakeet.

     _____

     _____

**CAPITALIZATION:**

1. "do you speak german, professor ritz?" asked miss lopez.


**PUNCTUATION:**

**Punctuate these titles:**

2. A. (book)    Roses for Mona

   B. (poem)   A Bird Came Walking down the Street

   C. (essay)   Every Dog Should Own a Man


**PARTS OF SPEECH:   ADJECTIVES**

**Circle the correct adjective:**

3. Of the five necklaces, this once is ( shinier, shiniest ).


**DIRECT OBJECTS:**

**Underline the subject once and the verb or verb phrase twice.  Label any direct object(s) – D.O.:**

4. The photographer took a picture.


**PHRASES/CLAUSES:**

**Write P if the group of words is a phrase; write C if the group of words is a clause:**

5. A. _____   In summary, voters should decide.

   B. _____   In the middle of the extremely hot afternoon.


**SENTENCE COMBINING:**

6. Give this note to the lady.
   The lady is taking tickets.
   The lady is tall.

   _____

   _____

**DAY 28**

**CAPITALIZATION:**

1.  mr. booth bought a  dogtooth violet, a north american flower, at targo plant nursery.

**PUNCTUATION:**

2.  Her mother in law was born on July 4 1947

**PARTS OF SPEECH:    NOUNS**

   **Write the possessive form:**

3.  A.  a parakeet belonging to one girl - _____

    B.  a parakeet belonging to two girls - _____

**LIBRARY SKILLS:**

4.  A reference book that contains maps is called a/an _____.

**SPELLING:**

   **A one-syllable word ending in consonant + vowel + consonant  (VCV) usually
   doubles the final consonant when adding a suffix beginning with a <u>vowel</u>.**
             Examples:   tan + ing  =  tanning          flat + en  =  flatten
   **Write the correct spelling of the following words:**

5.  A.  mat + ed - _____

    B.  prop + ed - _____

    C.  sad + ness - _____

**SENTENCE COMBINING:**

6.  Allison waved her hand excitedly.
    Allison hailed a taxi.
    Allison stepped into the street.

    _____

    _____

**CAPITALIZATION:**

1.  michael jordan led the chicago bulls to several national basketball association championships.

**PUNCTUATION:**

2.  Yeah   Peters uncle is coming

**PARTS OF SPEECH:    PRONOUNS**

   **Circle the correct pronoun:**

3.  The winner of the baby contest was ( he, him ).

**PARTS OF SPEECH:    PREPOSITIONS**

   **Circle any preposition:**

4.  at    and    until    above    his    here    from    before    except    in    for

**SPELLING:**

   **Write the correct spelling of the following words:**

5.  A.  stun + ing - _____

   B.  smirk + ed - _____

   C.  scan + er - _____

**SENTENCE COMBINING:**

6.  Peach cobbler was served.
   It was warm.
   It was served with vanilla ice cream.

   _____

   _____

**DAY 30**

**CAPITALIZATION:**

1.   "when i had measles, grammy remze and i played rummy," said leah.

**PUNCTUATION:**

2.   Please get the following change  nickels dimes and quarters

**PARTS OF SPEECH:    ADJECTIVES**

   **Some limiting adjectives tell *which one.***

   **Circle any limiting adjectives telling *which one*:**

3.   This cotton shirt is cooler than those rayon ones.

**ANTONYMS/HOMONYMS/SYNONYMS:**
   **Antonyms are words with opposite meanings.**
   **Synonyms are words with similar meanings.**
   **Homonyms are words that are spelled differently but sound alike.**

4.   A.   An antonym for *old* is _____.
     B.   A synonym for *old* is _____.

**SENTENCES/FRAGMENTS:**

**Write S if the group of words is a sentence; write F if the group of words is a fragment:**

5.   A.   _____   Art class late in the day.
     B.   _____   A heifer fed at a trough.

**SENTENCE COMBINING:**

6.   The brain weighs only three pounds.
     It has 400 thousand million nerve cells.

     _____

     _____

**CAPITALIZATION:**

1.  joy will be attending the national association of manufacturers' meeting.

**PUNCTUATION:**

2.  These houses by the way are small secluded ones

**PARTS OF SPEECH:**

**A regular verb adds ed to form both the past and past participle.**
                                    **past              past participle**
        Example:   to yell:   yelled      (has, have, had)  yelled

**An irregular verb does not form the past or past participle by adding ed.**
        Example:   to give:   gave        (has, have, had)  given

**Write RV if the verb is regular; write IV if the verb is irregular:**

3.  A. ____  to sneeze      C. ____  to pretend     E. ____  to live
    B. ____  to stand       D. ____  to do          F. ____  to like

**PARTS OF SPEECH:    PRONOUNS**
  **Circle the correct pronoun:**

4.  George and ( he, him ) will swim in a race.

**ANALOGIES:**
  **Circle the answer that best completes the analogy:**

5.  forgery : real :: flattery : _____
    (a) false      (b) blush      (c) criticism      (d) compliment

**SENTENCE COMBINING:**

6.  Her favorite food is chicken.
    She likes it marinated in mustard sauce.

    _____

    _____

**DAY 32**

**CAPITALIZATION:**

1.  the zimbo restaurant on crestview avenue features southern fried chicken and louisana red beans.


**PUNCTUATION:**

2.  The newly formed choir led by Mrs Lewis sang Home on the Range


**PARTS OF SPEECH:    ADVERBS**

   **Circle any adverbs telling *how*:**

3.  Jana hit the ball hard and ran fast to first base.


**PARTS OF SPEECH:    NOUNS**

   **Write C if the word is a common noun; write P if the noun is a proper noun:**

4.  A. _____  hospital           C. _____  tree           E. _____  dog
    B. _____  Taylor Hospital     D. _____  elm            F. _____  Lassie


**SPELLING:**

   **Write the correct spelling of the following words:**

5.  A.  gaze + ing - _____
    B.  strand + ed - _____
    C.  strap + ed - _____


**SENTENCE COMBINING:**

6.  He was hunting for his missing shoe.
    He found a five dollar bill.

    _____

    _____

**CAPITALIZATION:**

1.  they fished for yellow perch at davis creek reservoir in ord, nebraska.

**PUNCTUATION:**

2.  Mike do you take swimming lessons at the YMCA

**SENTENCE TYPES:**

   **Write the sentence type:**

3.  A.  Please pass this bread.  _____

    B.  My friend loves to read.  _____

    C.  You're right!  _____

**PARTS OF SPEECH:   VERBS**

   **Select the verb that agrees with the subject:**

4.  Those plumbers ( work, works ) long hours.

**ANALOGIES:**

   **Circle the answer that best completes the analogy:**

5.  tie : bind :: rise : _____
    (a) regain      (b) incense      (c) ascend      (d) obstruct

**SENTENCE COMBINING:**

6.  The first grader sounded out a word.
    Then, the first grader smiled at his father.

    _____

    _____

# DAY 34

## CAPITALIZATION:

1. on st. patrick's day, paul took route 206 to malheur national wildlife refuge.

## PUNCTUATION:

2. Ms Diaz is the ladies bowling team competing today

## PARTS OF SPEECH:   NOUNS

**Write C if the word is a concrete noun; write A if the noun is an abstract noun:**

3.  A. ____ water          C. ____ honesty          E. ____ scissors

    B. ____ respect        D. ____ plug             F. ____ freedom

## PARTS OF SPEECH:   ADJECTIVES/ADVERBS

**Circle the correct word:**

4. The carpet cleaner didn't shampoo the rug ( good, well ).

## SPELLING:

**Write the correct spelling of the following words:**

5.  A. price + less - _____

    B. pit + ed - _____

    C. relieve + ing - _____

## SENTENCE COMBINING:

6. Vikings launched raids in longboats.
   Longboats had one row of oars on each side.

   _____

   _____

**CAPITALIZATION:**

1.  ty cobb, the first baseball player elected to the national baseball hall of fame, stole 892 bases.

**PUNCTUATION:**

2.  The boys club will meet at 5 30 P M on Monday June 5th

**PARTS OF SPEECH:    NOUNS**

   **Write the plural of the following nouns:**

3.  A.  storm - _____      C.  table - _____      E.  speech -_____

    B.  man - _____        D.  ditch - _____      F.  deer - _____

**PARTS OF SPEECH:   VERBS**

   **Write the present tense and the past tense:**

                            *present*                          *past*
4.  A.  to scare - _____      _____

    B.  to follow - _____     _____

    C.  to eat - _____        _____

**ANALOGIES:**

   **Circle the answer that best completes the analogy:**

5.  part : component :: donor : _____
    (a) receiver      (b) disease      (c) blood      (d) giver

**SENTENCE COMBINING:**

6.  The English sparrow was introduced into the United States.
    It was introduced to fight cankerworms.

    _____

    _____

**DAY 36**

**CAPITALIZATION:**

1.   the road crew from straban township opened the chambersburg pike after the blizzard.


**PUNCTUATION:**

2.   Dear Deka
        Bring your new blue dress with you
                Love
                Sally

**PARTS OF SPEECH:   ADVERBS**

**Circle any adverbs that tell *where*:**

3.   The little boy looked up and fell down.


**PARTS OF SPEECH:    NOUNS**

**Nouns name persons, places, things, and ideas.**

**Circle any nouns:**

4.   An electrician installed a light in the garage.


**CATEGORIES:**
**Items can be classified in a number of ways.  Frequently, a list is given
and a heading is assigned to that list.**     Example:  <u>beverages</u>
                                           - lemonade
                                           - juice
**Write a heading for this list:**                    - soda

5.   _____
       -ring
       -bracelet
       -necklace


**SENTENCE COMBINING:**

6.   Stuffed bears were collected.
    Large red bows were attached.
    They were donated to a children's hospital.

_____

_____

**CAPITALIZATION:**

**Capitalize these lines of poetry by Percy Bysshe Shelley:**

1.  music, when soft voices die,

    vibrates in the memory--

**PUNCTUATION:**

2.  This half filled balloon most certainly needs more air Micah

**PARTS OF SPEECH:    PREPOSITIONS**

**Circle any preposition:**

3.  from    or    of    with    bring    across    beyond    after    in    off

**DICTIONARY:    ALPHABETIZING**

**Place the following words in alphabetical order:**  system, sack, mental, nearby, metal, sea

4.  (a) _____    (c) _____    (e) _____

    (b) _____    (d) _____    (f) _____

**CATEGORIES:**

**Items can be classified in a number of ways.  Sometimes, items are listed under a heading.**

**Write a list:**

5.  sports

        -_____
        -_____
        -_____

**SENTENCE COMBINING:**

6.  Warfare was common in Europe during the Middle Ages.
    Castles were built for protection.

    _____

    _____

**DAY 38**

**CAPITALIZATION:**

1.  after shopping at rubio's department store, mom will take us to greenbelt park.


**PUNCTUATION:**

2.  Roy said  Ive lost my keys and my wallet


**PARTS OF SPEECH:**
   **Write the present tense and past tense:**
   *present*                                    *past*

3.  A.  to decide - _____        _____

    B.  to run - _____        _____

    C.  to see - _____        _____

    D.  to play - _____        _____


**PARTS OF SPEECH:    ADJECTIVES**
   **Some adjectives limit rather than describe.**

4.  A.  The three articles are _____, _____, and _____.

    B.  The four demonstrative adjectives that begin with *th* are_____,

        _____, _____, and _____.


**ANALOGIES:**

   **Circle the answer that best completes the analogy:**

5.  admit : confess :: abbreviate : _____
    (a)  shorten        (b)  word        (c)  dictionary        (d)  create


**SENTENCE COMBINING:**

6.  Melissa likes to read mysteries.
    Carli likes to read science fiction.

    _____

    _____

**CAPITALIZATION:**

1. a baptist church held a christian film series in february.

**PUNCTUATION:**

2. The childrens playground is located at 27 Swan Drive Hillsborough NC   27278

**PARTS OF SPEECH:**

**Circle the correct pronoun:**

3. Mario's dad and ( we, us ) are designing a house.

**PHRASES/CLAUSES:**

**Write P if the group of words is a phrase; write C if the group of words is a clause:**

4. A. _____ In the basement

   B. _____ When her brother laughed

**SPELLING:**

**Write the correct spelling of the following words:**

5. A. dim + ly - _____

   B. scar + ed - _____

   C. react + ion - _____

**SENTENCE COMBINING:**

6. Magpies are scavengers.
   They often collect small objects.
   The objects are also bright.

   _____

   _____

**DAY 40**

**CAPITALIZATION:**

1. dr. parks and dad played golf at lemon tree golf club on memorial day.


**PUNCTUATION:**
   **Punctuate these titles:**

2. A. (magazine)   Exercise World

   B. (magazine article)   How to Play Outfield

   C. (book)   Gold Rush Prodigal


**SUBJECT/VERB:**
   **Compound verb means more than one.**

   **Underline the subject once and the verb twice:**

3. The rodeo cowboy lassoed the steer and quickly tied it.


**LIBRARY:**

4. What book provides synonyms? _____


**ANALOGIES:**
   **The first word of an analogy may express a general topic, and the second word may state a type/category of that topic. Select the answer that has the same relationship to the third word.**
   Meat : beef :: drink : _____
   (a) beverage   **(b) lemonade**   (c) straw   (d) dinner

   **Circle the answer that best completes the analogy:**

5. fish : trout :: bear : _____
   (a) cub   (b) grizzly   (c) woods   (d) salmon


**SENTENCE COMBINING:**

6. We called our grandmother.
   She was painting her house.

   _____

   _____

**CAPITALIZATION:**

1.  have you, mom, visited majesty tower gardens in florida?

**PUNCTUATION:**

**Punctuate this outline:**

2.  I   Literature

> A   Prose

>> 1   Plays

>> 2   Novels

> B   Poetry

**PARTS OF SPEECH:    ADVERBS**

**Circle any adverbs that tell *to what extent*:**

3.  A very elderly man stood rather still.

**PREFIXES/ROOTS/SUFFIXES:**

4.  The root word of undone is _____.

**ANALOGIES:**

**Circle the answer that best completes the analogy:**

5.  footwear : moccasin :: barrier : _____
    (a) vent      (b) barrel      (c) wall      (d) envy

**SENTENCE COMBINING:**

6.  They laid tile in their entryway.
    They placed carpeting in their living room.
    They put linoleum in their kitchen.

    _____

    _____

**DAY 42**

**CAPITALIZATION:**

1.   a rare member of bighorn sheep lives in the sierra madre mountains of the west.

**PUNCTUATION:**

2.   Have Mrs Minter and Capt Brewer presented an award to the citys mayor

**PARTS OF SPEECH:     INTERJECTIONS**

   **Circle the interjection:**

3.   Yippee!  It's time to start!

**PARTS OF SPEECH:     PRONOUNS**

   **Circle the correct pronoun:**

4.   The barber gave ( they, them ) combs.

**ANALOGIES:**

   **Circle the answer that best completes the analogy:**

5.   flower : carnation :: fabric : _____
     (a)  clothing       (b)  corduroy       (c)  softener       (d)  shirt

**SENTENCE COMBINING:**

6.   There are three species of kiwi birds.
     All three species are protected.

     _____

     _____

**CAPITALIZATION:**

1.  naomi asked, "are penquins only found in antarctica?"

**PUNCTUATION:**

2.  Jan Clark D D S cant be here today

**PARTS OF SPEECH:    PREPOSITIONS**

   **Circle any object of the preposition:**

3.  The man with his bag fled into the street.

**PARTS OF SPEECH:    VERBS**

   **Write the contraction:**

4.  A.  does not - _____      D.  they are - _____

    B.  she is - _____      E.  had not - _____

    C.  I will - _____      F.  here is - _____

**SPELLING:**

   **Write the correct spelling of the following words:**

5.  A.  fool + ish - _____      C.  degrade + ing - _____

    B.  gnash + ed - _____      D.  slat + ed - _____

**SENTENCE COMBINING:**

6.  The father rocked the baby.
    He sang to the baby at the same time.

    _____

    _____

**DAY 44**

**CAPITALIZATION:**

1.  was the famous ship, <u>r. m. s. titanic</u>, built in belfast, ireland?

**PUNCTUATION:**

2.  That small chubby baby wont come to me

**PARTS OF SPEECH:    ADVERBS**

  **Circle any adverbs that tell *when*:**

3.  Brian often plays chess, and he never seems to lose.

**SUBJECT/VERB:**

  **Cross out any prepositional phrases.  Underline the subject once and the verb or verb phrase twice:**

4.  At the picnic, some people were playing volleyball.

**SPELLING:**
  **Words ending in consonant + <u>y</u> usually change the <u>y</u> to <u>i</u> before adding a suffix beginning with a vowel; <u>es</u> is added in the present tense.  However, words ending in <u>y</u> do not drop the <u>y</u> to add <u>ing</u>.**
  Examples:   hurry + s = hurr**ies**        hurrying + ing  =  hurrying

  **Write the correct spelling of the following words:**

5.  A.  steady + ed - _____

    B.  steady + s - _____

    C.  steady + ing - _____

**SENTENCE COMBINING:**

6.  The child was dirty from playing in the dirt.
    She did not want to take a bath.

    _____

    _____

**CAPITALIZATION:**

1.  in 1928, the kiwanis club gave funds to abbeville-greenwood regional library.

**PUNCTUATION:**
  **Punctuate this address:**
2.  _____

                                    Ms Sarah I Thorpe
                                    5712 E Penny Lane
                                    Tacoma WA    98408

  _____

**PARTS OF SPEECH:   NOUNS**
  **Write A if the noun is abstract; write C if the noun is concrete:**

3.  A. _____ clock       C. _____ sincerity     E. _____ air
    B. _____ beauty      D. _____ sauce         F. _____ nervousness

**PARTS OF SPEECH:   ADJECTIVES**
  **Write the proper adjective:**

4.  A.  a (Japan) garden        _____
    B.  a (Franklin) invention  _____
    C.  an (England) writer     _____

**SENTENCES:**
  **A clause contains a subject and a verb.**
  **A clause may express a complete thought.  This is called an independent clause.**
      Example:   He has blisters on his foot.
  **A clause may not express a complete thought.  This is called a dependent clause.**
      Example:  When his mother had a virus
  **Write DC if the clause is dependent; write IC if the clause is independent:**

5.  A.  _____    After they were falsely accused of a crime.

    B.  _____    She greeted her brother warmly.

**SENTENCE COMBINING:**

6.  The window is in the hallway.
    It has roses on it.
    The window is round.

  _____

  _____

**DAY 46**

**CAPITALIZATION:**

1. the agency, osha,* was established within the department of labor in 1970.

*Occupational Safety and Health Administration

**PUNCTUATION:**

2. Yes my grandpa Julian S Rios lives nearby

**PARTS OF SPEECH:    CONJUNCTIONS**
   **Circle any conjunctions in the following sentence:**

3. This cat looks meek, but he bites.

**FRIENDLY LETTER:**
   **Label the parts of this friendly letter: (A) body   (B) signature   (C) heading**
   **(D) salutation (greeting)    (E) closing**

4.                                  ( )            891 North 52<sup>nd</sup> Lane
                                                   Marietta, GA   30066
                                                   October 21, 20—
   ( )      Dear Lulu,
   ( )           Your grandmother and I have just returned from a trip to California.
            We went to Bay Harbor in San Diego and to Cole's Farm near Retroland.
                                  ( )                      Love,
                                  ( )                      Grandpa Begay

**SPELLING:**
   **Write the correct spelling of the following words:**

5.  A.  haste + y - _____

    B.  hurt + ing - _____

    C.  stir + ed - _____

**SENTENCE COMBINING:**

6.  A potto is an animal.
    It has wooly fur.
    It lives in Africa.

    _____

    _____

**CAPITALIZATION:**

1. the herb, safflower, grown in southern asia, is a source of cooking oil.

**PUNCTUATION:**

2. If you arent going lets play table tennis

**PARTS OF SPEECH:    ADVERBS**

   **Circle the correct answer:**

3. Of the three men on motorcycles, Heyward reacts ( more quickly, most quickly ).

**LIBRARY:    REFERENCE**

4. A reference book that provides *current* information and statistics is a/an

   _____.

**ANALOGIES:**

   **Analogies may express part to a whole.  The first word states a part; the second word states the entire item to which the first word belongs.   The second set must show the same relationship.**

   Finger : hand :: toe : _____
   (a) nail   **(b) foot**   (c) leg   (d) ankle

   **Circle the answer that best completes the analogy:**

5. mattress : crib :: blade : _____
   (a) fan   (b) fork   (c) turn   (d) cooling

**SENTENCE COMBINING:**

6. Emma is a lawyer.
   Emma wants to have her own law firm.

   _____

   _____

**DAY 48**

**CAPITALIZATION:**

1. after a tour of st. paul's cathedral in london, they went to hyde park.

**PUNCTUATION:**

2. In the car seat yourself by the back window

**PARTS OF SPEECH:    ADJECTIVES**

   **Circle the correct adjective:**

3. This swimsuit is ( gooder, better ) than mine.

**SUBJECT/VERB:**

   **Cross out any prepositional phrases.  Underline the subject once and the verb or verb phrase twice:**

4. Miss Valentino and her grandmother have arrived at the airport.

**SPELLING:**

   **Write the correct spelling of the following words:**

5. A.  receive + ing - _____

   B.  bat + er - _____

   C.  taste + ful - _____

**SENTENCE COMBINING:**

6. The circus is coming to town.
   I cannot attend.

   _____

   _____

**CAPITALIZATION:**

1. the city of doha on the persian gulf in southeast arabia was once a fishing village.

**PUNCTUATION:**

2. Shawn graduated in 92 in Hanover Pennsylvania

**PARTS OF SPEECH:    ADVERBS**

Circle any adverbs that tell *where* or *when*:

3. Recently, he went downtown to purchase new tires.

**DICTIONARY:    GUIDE WORDS**

**Guide Words            pirate        pretty**

Will the following words be found on a dictionary page with the guide words, *pirate* and *pretty*?  Write Yes or No in the blank:

4.  A.  _____  pint          C.  _____  private

    B.  _____  pillow        D.  _____  pneumonia

**SPELLING:**

Write the correct spelling of these words:

5.  A.  recluse + ive  - _____

    B.  wrap + ed - _____

    C.  dent + ed - _____

**SENTENCE COMBINING:**

6.  Hudson Stuck was the first to climb Mt. McKinley.
    Mt. McKinley is in Alaska.
    He did this in 1913.

    _____

    _____

**DAY 50**

**CAPITALIZATION:**

1.  the federalist party was started by alexander hamilton.

**PUNCTUATION:**
   **Punctuate these titles:**

2.  A.  (book)    Inside of the Blue Dolphins

    B.  (movie)    My Side of the Mountain

    C.  (magazine)    Animal Journal

    D.  (magazine article)    Seven Ways to Help Your Child

**PARTS OF SPEECH:**
   **Write <u>Yes</u> if the word adds *es* to form the plural; write <u>No</u> if it does not:**

3.  A.  _____  crash        C.  _____  trick        E.  _____  trench

    B.  _____  mint         D.  _____  floss        F.  _____  relax

**ANTONYMS/HOMONYMS/SYNONYMS:**

4.  A.  An antonym for *fickle* is _____.

    B.  A homonym for *straight* is _____.

    C.  A synonym for *consume* is _____.

**ANALOGIES:**

   **Circle the answer that best completes the analogy:**

5.  buckle : belt :: latch  : _____
    (a) gate        (b) opening    (c) bridge    (d) iron

**SENTENCE COMBINING:**

6.  Kami is placing dishes in a box.
    The boxes are moving boxes.
    She is wrapping her dishes in newspaper.

   _____

   _____

**CAPITALIZATION:**

1. the butcher's shop is south of pebble shoe co. on royal street.

**PUNCTUATION:**

**Punctuate this heading and greeting of a friendly letter:**

2.                                                       12 West Palm Lane
                                                         Burger TX  79007
                                                         April 9  20—

    Dear Stan

**LIBRARY:**

3. Books that are not true are called _____.

**PARTS OF SPEECH:    NOUNS**

**Write the possessive:**

4. A. a truck belonging to a woman - _____

    B. a club belonging to five boys - _____

    C. shoes belonging to children - _____

**SPELLING:**

**Words that end in vowel + _y_ usually do not change when adding a suffix.**

    Examples:   ray + s  =  rays        decay + ing  =  decaying

**Write the correct spelling of these words:**

5. A. donkey + s - _____

    B. relay + ed - _____

    C. deny + ed - _____

**SENTENCE COMBINING:**

6. Ravens can be found in the icy Arctic.
    They can also be found in the warm regions of the Northern Hemisphere.

    _____

    _____

**DAY 52**

**CAPITALIZATION:**

1.  "will the animal welfare league meet at phoenix civic plaza on adams street?" asked dee.

**PUNCTUATION:**

2.  Rick dot your i in the first word of your paragraph

**DIFFICULT WORDS:**
   **Circle the correct word:**

3.  A.  This sticky bun is ( to, too, two ) gooey.

    B.  ( Your, You're ) right!

    C.  ( There, Their, They're ) are only five candles on the cake.

**PARTS OF SPEECH:    ADJECTIVES**
   **Indefinites can be determiners.  Some indefinites are *some, few, many, several, no,* and *any.*  When an indefinite appears in a sentence, check to determine if it modifies (goes over to) a noun or a pronoun.**
      Example:    **Several** *swans* swam with **many** *ducks.*

   **Circle any determining adjective and box what it modifies:**

4.  We scored fewer points in the final game.

**SENTENCES/FRAGMENTS/RUN-ONS:**

   **Write <u>S</u> if the group of words is a sentence; write <u>F</u> if the group of words is a fragment:**

5.  A.  _____    The man who just left.

    B.  _____    You're tall.

**SENTENCE COMBINING:**

6.  The carpenter picked up lumber.
    He turned to talk to the foreman at the same time.

   _____

   _____

**CAPITALIZATION:**

1.  on saturday mornings, dad buys rolls at brighton bakery on regal avenue.

**PUNCTUATION:**

 **Write the abbreviation:**

2.  A.  mountains - _____          D.  before Christ - _____

 B.  Tuesday - _____          E.  August - _____

 C.  company - _____          F.  boulevard - _____

**PARTS OF SPEECH:   PRONOUNS**

 **Circle the correct pronoun:**

3.  Blake and ( her, she ) talked on the telephone.

**PARTS OF SPEECH:   ADJECTIVES/ADVERBS**

 **Circle the correct word:**

4.  Hannah is a good swimmer.  Hannah swims ( good, well ).

**ANALOGIES:**

 **Circle the answer that best completes the analogy:**

5.  ask : inquire :: sink : _____
 (a) emerge     (b) float     (c) avert     (d) submerge

**SENTENCE COMBINING:**

6.  Mr. Ving returns all phone calls.
 He does this every day.
 He does it after he eats lunch.

 _____

 _____

**DAY 54**

**CAPITALIZATION:**

1.  does the receptionist at luana beach resort hotel speak russian?

**PUNCTUATION:**

2.  He was born on Thurs Mar 26 1992 in Miami Florida

**SUBJECT/VERB:**

   **Underline the subject once and the verb or verb phrase twice:**

3.  Are the cups and saucers on the bottom shelf?

**PARTS OF SPEECH:    NOUNS**

4.  A.   Write an example of a common noun: _____

    B.   Write an example of a proper noun: _____

**SPELLING:**

   **Write the correct spelling of these words:**

5.  A.  bully + ed - _____

    B.  grace + ful - _____

    C.  reside + ing - _____

**SENTENCE COMBINING:**

6.  Lungfish live in the rivers of South America.
    Lungfish live in the rivers of Africa.
    Lungfish live in the rivers of Australia.

   _____

   _____

**CAPITALIZATION:**

1.   the first olympic games were held in rome in 776 b. c.


**PUNCTUATION:**
   **Punctuate these titles:**

2.   A.   (newspaper)   Morning Tribune          C.   (song)   Winter Wonderland

      B.   (chapter)   Westward Expansion        D.   (magazine)   Travel Delight


**SENTENCE TYPES:**
   **Write the sentence type:**

3.   A.   _____   Are you lost?

      B.   _____   Sit down, please.

      C.   _____   This oatmeal tastes great.


**PARTS OF SPEECH:   VERBS**
   **Write RV if the verb is regular; write IV if the verb is irregular:**

4.   A.   ____   to slide       C.   ____   to cry       E.   ____   to draw

      B.   ____   to visit       D.   ____   to go        F.   ____   to write


**ANALOGIES:**

   **Circle the answer that best completes the analogy:**

5.   rungs : ladder :: petals : _____
      (a)  flower       (b)  stamen       (c)  bulbs       (d)  pollination


**SENTENCE COMBINING:**

6.   The colt struggled to its feet.
      It was a newborn colt.
      The colt rose shakily.

      _____

      _____

**DAY 56**

**CAPITALIZATION:**

1. many workers on the panama canal developed a disease called malaria.

**PUNCTUATION:**

**Punctuate this heading, greeting, closing, and signature of a friendly letter:**

2.
                                          37 Osborn Road
                                          San Antonio TX  79007
                                          Dec 27  20—

       Dear Luana

                                          Your aunt
                                          Chessa

**DICTIONARY:    ALPHABETIZING**

**Place the following words in alphabetical order:**  elegant, cord, float, egg, harbor, east

3.   (a) _____      (c) _____      (e) _____
     (b) _____      (d) _____      (f) _____

**PARTS OF SPEECH:    NOUNS**

**Circle any nouns in the following sentence:**

4.   At the raceway, two cars crossed the line at the same time.

**ANALOGIES:**

**Analogies may express whole to part.  The first word states the item, and the second word states a part.  The second set must show the same relationship.**

**Circle the answer that best completes the analogy:**

5.   stool : seat : omelet : _____
     (a) souffle      (b) egg      (c) breakfast      (d) waffle

**SENTENCE COMBINING:**

6.   Carlo usually goes to bed at midnight.
     Carlo usually takes out the garbage before that.

     _____

     _____

**CAPITALIZATION:**

1.   the u. s. department of health and human services is concerned about aging problems.

**PUNCTUATION:**

2.   Their boys club is at 212 Fee Street Bend Oregon  97702

**PARTS OF SPEECH:   NOUNS**

   **Write the plural:**

3.   A.   oven - _____          D.   mouse - _____

     B.   boy - _____            E.   moose - _____

     C.   baby - _____           F.   half - _____

**PARTS OF SPEECH:   VERBS**

   **Note:   Crossing out any prepositional phrases will help to determine subject.**

   **Select the verb that agrees with the subject:**

4.   One of the magazines ( are, is ) on the table.

**SPELLING:**

   **Write the correct spelling of the following words:**

5.   A.   precise + ly - _____

     B.   dread + ing - _____

     C.   desire + ous - _____

**SENTENCE COMBINING:**

6.   That barn is old.
     It is used to store equipment.
     The equipment is used for the farm.

     _____

     _____

**DAY 58**

**CAPITALIZATION:**

1.   in the 1840's, many roman catholic immigrants settled in eastern cities.

**PUNCTUATION:**

2.   On July 4 1776 Americas independence was declared

**PARTS OF SPEECH:   PREPOSITIONS**

   **Circle prepositions:**

3.   along    below    out      concerning    doubt    inside    through    up
     within   or       my       regarding     since    beside    belong     no
     past     too      down     against       toward   into      himself    in

**PARTS OF SPEECH:   VERBS (with *not*)**

   **Select the correct word:**

4.   That teller ( don't, doesn't ) know all the customers.

**SENTENCES/FRAGMENTS/RUN-ONS:**

**Write S for sentence; write F for fragment:**

5.   A.   _____    The man in the dinner jacket is giving a speech.

     B.   _____    Because he was playing in several mud puddles.

**SENTENCE COMBINING:**

6.   Tourism makes the country of Aruba prosper.
     Oil refining makes Aruba prosper.
     Financial dealings make Aruba prosper.

   _____

   _____

**CAPITALIZATION:**
  **Capitalize this outline:**

1.   i.   flying insects

     a.   harmful ones

          1.   insects that spread diseases

          2.   poisonous insects

     b.   harmless ones

**PUNCTUATION:**

2.   Towels shirts and pants lay in a knee deep heap on the floor

**PARTS OF SPEECH:**

  **The prefix de means away or away from.**

3.   A.   Explain the meaning of *detour*. _____

     B.   What is the root (base) word of *detour*? _____

**PARTS OF SPEECH:    ADVERBS**

  **Circle any adverbs that tell *where*:**

4.   Tina fished upstream while Lindsey and Jim sat on the banks to read.

**SPELLING:**

  **Write the correct spelling of the following words:**

5.   A.   invent + ive - _____

     B.   pastry + s - _____

     C.   volley + s - _____

**SENTENCE COMBINING:**

6.   The doctor put eight stitches in her hand.
     The doctor then explained how to care for stitches.

     _____

     _____

**DAY 60**

**CAPITALIZATION:**

1.  the brawner family attends the strawberry folk festival held in the south.

**PUNCTUATION:**

2.  J F Kennedy was assassinated in Dallas Texas on November 22 1963

**PARTS OF SPEECH:    ADJECTIVES**

   **Circle any descriptive adjectives:**

3.  Her long brown hair blew in the gentle breeze.

**PARTS OF SPEECH:    VERBS**

   **Underline the verb phrase twice:**

4.  The athlete should not have ( threw, thrown ) the ball so hard.

**ANALOGIES:**

   **Circle the answer that best completes the analogy:**

5.  admit : confess :: pacify : _____
    (a) soothe      (b) anger      (c) pace      (d) affirm

**SENTENCE COMBINING:**

6.  Charles M. Schulz was an American cartoonist.
    He created the Peanuts comic strip.

   _____

   _____

**CAPITALIZATION:**

1.                                                      7891 west crocus drive
                                                        mission viejo, ca   92692
                                                        jan. 31, 20—

   dear aunt grace,


                                                        sincerely yours,
                                                        wilma

**PUNCTUATION:**

2.   The short funny lady bought twenty seven balloons for the party

**PARTS OF SPEECH:    VERBS**

   **Write the future tense of the following verbs:**

3.   A.   to seem - _____
     B.   to fall - _____

**PARTS OF SPEECH:    PRONOUNS**

   **Circle the correct pronoun:**

4.   The teacher gave ( us, we ) students a prize.

**ANALOGIES:**

   **Circle the answer that best completes the analogy:**

5.   computer : monitor :: pump  : _____
       (a)  air      (b)  machine    (c)  tires     (d)  handle

**SENTENCE COMBINING:**

6.   Mahogany is a hard wood.
     It resists termites.

     _____

     _____

**DAY 62**

**CAPITALIZATION:**

1. their tour of iceland included vatnajokull, the largest glacier in europe.

**PUNCTUATION:     PRONOUNS**

2. You without a doubt dont want this half eaten sandwich

**PARTS OF SPEECH:**

   **Circle the correct pronoun:**

3. To ( who, whom ) did I give my paper?

**SUBJECT/VERB:**

   **Cross out any prepositional phrases.  Underline the subject once and the verb or verb phrase twice:**

4. An army of ants marched silently across the brick walkway.

**SYNONYMS/ANTONYMS:**
   **Write <u>Syn</u>. if the words are synonyms; write <u>Ant</u>. if the words are antonyms:**

5. A. _____     obey – violate
   B. _____     return – confiscate
   C. _____     natural – organic

**SENTENCE COMBINING:**

6. The plate is antique.
   It is trimmed in gold.
   It has a small rose on its center.
   The rose is pink.

   _____

   _____

**CAPITALIZATION:**

1.  was sarah caldwell the first woman to conduct the metropolitan opera?

**PUNCTUATION:**
  **Write the abbreviation:**

2.  A.  Sunday - _____       E.  Thursday - _____

   B.  Monday - _____         F.  Friday - _____

   C.  Tuesday - _____          G.  Saturday - _____

   D.  Wednesday - _____

**PARTS OF SPEECH:   PRONOUNS**

3.  The objective pronouns are _____, _____, _____, _____, _____,
     _____, _____, and _____.

**PARTS OF SPEECH:   ADVERBS**

  **Circle any adverbs that tell *to what extent*:**

4.  "I'm not too tired to play," said Karen.

**SENTENCES:**
  **A clause contains a subject and a verb.**
  **A clause may express a complete thought.  This is called an independent clause.**
    Example:   They <u>looked</u> at a map.
  **A clause may not express a complete thought.  This is called a dependent clause.**
    Example:   Before <u>Dad</u> <u>called</u> home

  **Write <u>DC</u> if the clause is dependent; write <u>IC</u> if the clause is independent:**

5.  A.  _____     After they were falsely accused of a crime.

   B.  _____     She greeted her brother warmly.

**SENTENCE COMBINING:**
6.  Balsamic vinegar is made from the must of white grapes.
    It is an aged Italian vinegar.

   _____

   _____

**DAY 64**

**CAPITALIZATION:**

1.   pets are allowed on pacific crest trail in north cascades national park.

**PUNCTUATION:**
   **Write the abbreviation for each month.  If there is no abbreviation, write the name of the month:**

2.   A.   January - _____     E.   May - _____     I.   September - _____

   B.   February - _____     F.   June - _____     J.   October - _____

   C.   March - _____     G.   July - _____     K.   November - _____

   D.   April - _____     H.   August - _____     L.   December - _____

**PARTS OF SPEECH:     VERBS**
   **Cross out any prepositional phrases.  Underline the subject once and the verb or verb phrase twice:**

3.   A nurse studied the chart and talked to the patient.

**LIBRARY:**

4.   A.   The three types of cards in a card catalog are _____, _____, and _____.
   B.   Ju refers to *juvenile*.  What does this mean about a book? _____

**SPELLING:**
   **Words ending in consonant + consonant + e (CCe) usually drop the e when adding a suffix beginning with a vowel.  Example:  rinse + ing = rinsing   cuddle + ed = cuddle**

   **Write the correct spelling of these words:**

5.   A.   whistle + ing - _____

   B.   fence + ed - _____

   C.   resource + ful - _____

**SENTENCE COMBINING:**

6.   Pierre likes to scuba dive.
     His sister likes to snorkel.

   _____

   _____

**CAPITALIZATION:**

1.  did geronimo, the chiricahua apache leader, become a friend of president teddy roosevelt?

**PUNCTUATION:**

2.  Youre extremely efficient  said Mr Elton to the mechanic

**PARTS OF SPEECH:    ADVERBS**

  **Circle any adverbs that tell *how*:**

3.  Bobbie walked carefully but fast on the hot cement.

**PARTS OF SPEECH:    PRONOUNS**

  **Circle the correct pronoun:**

4.  The matter is between Ned and ( I, me ).

**SPELLING:**

  **Write the correct spelling of these words:**

5.  A.  bubble + ing - _____

    B.  response + ive - _____

    C.  reprise + al - _____

**SENTENCE COMBINING:**

6.  The little girl is helping to plant a garden.
    She is helping her aunt.
    She is placing water in each hole.

    _____

    _____

**DAY 66**

**CAPITALIZATION:**

1.  the lute, a popular musical instrument during the middle ages, has a pear-shaped body.

**PUNCTUATION:**

2.  Mentor Company Inc
    24 Zuni Hills Rd
    Sonoma CA    95370

    Ladies and Gentlemen of the Board

**PARTS OF SPEECH:    ADJECTIVES/NOUNS**

Write <u>A</u> if the boldfaced word serves as an adjective; write <u>N</u> if the boldfaced word serves as a noun:

3.  A.  _____     A fly is crawling on the **ceiling**.

    B.  _____     Turn on the **ceiling** fan, please.

**PARTS OF SPEECH:    ADVERBS**

Circle the correct form:

4.  Of the three mice, the white one acts ( more strangely, most strangely ).

**ANALOGIES:**

Circle the answer that best completes the analogy:

5.  shape : oval :: artwork : _____
    (a) watercolor      (b) artist      (c) museum      (d) sculptor

**SENTENCE COMBINING:**

6.  The ermine is called a short-tailed weasel in North America.
    The ermine was called a stoat in the Old World.

    _____

    _____

**CAPITALIZATION:**
   **Capitalize these titles:**

1. A. <u>cloud jewel</u>

   B. "a dutch picture"

   C. <u>love finds a home</u>

**PUNCTUATION:**

2. Yeah  Were leaving on the Super Chief a famous train

**PARTS OF SPEECH:    VERBS**

   **Select the correct verb:**

3. Neither Janell nor Mary ( has, have ) been chosen.

**PARTS OF SPEECH:    VERBS**

   **Write the contraction:**

4. A. I shall - _____          D. it is - _____

   B. will not - _____          E. have not - _____

   C. we are - _____          F. there is - _____

**PHRASES/CLAUSES:**

   **Write <u>P</u> if the group of words is a phrase; write <u>C</u> if the group of words is a clause:**

5. A. _____     Waving his hand.

   B. _____     She sat up.

**SENTENCE COMBINING:**

6. Lauren leaves for work at six each morning.
   She first packs a lunch.

   _____

   _____

**DAY 68**

**CAPITALIZATION:**

1.  in 1814, the british sent troops to the gulf of mexico to protect new orleans.

**PUNCTUATION:**

2.  My sister in law and Miss Gorham introduced us to Nancy Reese a newspaper reporter

**PARTS OF SPEECH:    INTERJECTIONS**
   **Write a sentence containing an interjection:**

3.  _____

    _____


**PARTS OF SPEECH:    ADJECTIVES**
   **Circle any proper adjectives in the following sentence:**

4.  The store carries Columbian coffee and British biscuits.

**CLAUSES:**
   **Write <u>DC</u> if the clause is dependent; write <u>IC</u> if the clause is independent:**

   **Remember:    A dependent clause does not express a complete thought.
   An independent  clause expresses a complete thought.**

5.  A.  _____    After we finished supper.
    B.  _____    She eased the sputtering car off the highway.

**SENTENCE COMBINING:**

6.  The tree is blooming.
    It is filled with white blossoms.
    The blossoms are fragrant.

    _____

    _____

**CAPITALIZATION:**

1.   the han gou canal was constructed in the city of chi near the modern city of bejing.

**PUNCTUATION:**
   **Punctuate the following:**

2.  A.  (train)   Silver Express          D.  (book)   Collected Poems

    B.  (magazine)   Rural Life          E.  (poem)   Travel

    C.  (magazine article)   Phoning Home

**PARTS OF SPEECH:     CONJUNCTIONS**

3.   The three common coordinating conjunctions are _____, _____,
     and _____.

**ALPHABETIZING:**

   **Write these words in alphabetical order:**   print, prior, permit, oboe, prince, obtain

4.   (a) _____          (d) _____

     (b) _____          (e) _____

     (c) _____          (f) _____

**SPELLING:**

   **Write the correct spelling of these words:**

5.   A.   positive + ly - _____

     B.   huffy + est - _____

     C.   trend + y - _____

**SENTENCE COMBINING:**

6.   Bobsledding has been an Olympic event since 1924.
     That is when the first Winter Games were held.

     _____

     _____

**DAY 70**

**CAPITALIZATION:**

1.  the fast japanese train called <u>shinkansen</u> travels at 200 miles per hour.

**PUNCTUATION:**

2.  Brett your two sons stained striped shirts cant be washed

**PARTS OF SPEECH:    NOUNS**

   **Write <u>A</u> if the noun is abstract; write <u>C</u> if the noun is concrete:**

3.  A.  ____    lamp         C.  ____    courage       E.  ____    socks

    B.  ____    hope         D.  ____    plastic        F.  ____    fog

**LIBRARY:**

4.  The *Readers' Guide to Periodical Literature* helps to find _____.

**ANALOGIES:**

   **Analogies may express an item to its purpose.  The first word states the item; the second word states its purpose.  The second set must also show this relationship.**

   needle : sewing :: saw : _____
   (a) construction    (b) jigsaw    **(c) cutting**    (d) fuse

   **Circle the answer that best completes the analogy:**

5.  towel : drying :: siren : _____
    (a) reprisal    (b) ambulance    (c) inquiry    (d) warning

**SENTENCE COMBINING:**

6.  His grandfather's friend was in World War II.
    He was in the U. S. Army.
    He was part of the Normandy Invasion.

    _____

    _____

**CAPITALIZATION:**

1.  walter perry johnson was a pitcher for the washington senators from 1907-1927.

**PUNCTUATION:**

2.  On Friday May 27 2012 his class will be graduating

**SENTENCES/FRAGMENTS:**
  **If the group of words is a complete sentence, write <u>S</u>; if the group of words isn't a complete sentence (fragment), write <u>F</u>:**

3.  A.  _____  They stood in line for tickets.

    B.  _____  Standing in line.

    C.  _____  If you have to stand in line.

**LIBRARY:**

4.  A _____ dictionary gives information about famous people.

**SPELLING:**

  **Write the correct spelling of these words:**

5.  A.  unseem + ly - _____

    B.  horrify + ed - _____

    C.  horrify + ing - _____

**SENTENCE COMBINING:**

6.  The end of a nerve cell sends impulses to other cells.
    It is called an axon.

    _____

    _____

**DAY 72**

**CAPITALIZATION:**

1. did you know that hiawatha national forest touches on three of the great lakes?

**PUNCTUATION:**

2. No Im not upset disturbed or angry

**PARTS OF SPEECH:    VERBS**

Underline the verb phrase twice:

3. A.  This bread has not ( risen, raised ).
   B.  Jordan was ( lying, laying ) on the floor.
   C.  You could have ( sat, set ) the box here.

**FRIENDLY LETTER:**
Label the parts of this friendly letter: **(A) body   (B) closing   (C) salutation (greeting)   (D) signature   (E) heading**

4.                                    ( )        2457 Meadow Lane
                                                 Winfield, KS  67156
                                                 October 24, 20—

   ( )    Dear Doug,
   ( )              What a great time we had trout fishing in Pennsylvania; the
          streams are perfect.  I'll see you soon for our next trip in Canada.
                               ( )              Yours truly,
                               ( )              Daryl

**ANALOGIES:**

Circle the answer that best completes the analogy:

5. watch : time :: compass : _____
   (a) direction      (b) needle      (c) apparatus      (d) measurement

**SENTENCE COMBINING:**

6. The apartment is on the third floor.
   The apartment is small.
   The apartment is perfect for the young couple.

   _____

   _____

**CAPITALIZATION:**

1.  developed as a german breed by louis doberman, the doberman pincher is sometimes used as a police dog.

**PUNCTUATION:**

2.  The A M A* held a doctors conference at 6 30 P M

*initials for American Medical Association

**PARTS OF SPEECH:    ADJECTIVES/ADVERBS**
   **Circle the correct word:**

3.  This technician does his job quite (good, well) on a daily basis.

**WORDS:**
   **Circle the correct word:**

4.   A.  ( Their, They're, There ) basket is on the table.

   B.  ( It's, Its ) tail wagged happily.

   C.  ( We're, Were ) planning a surprise party.

   D.  I like ( you're, your ) shoes.

**CLAUSES:**
   **Write DC if the clause is dependent; write IC if the clause is independent:**
   **Remember:    A clause contains a subject and a verb.**
   **An independent  clause expresses a complete thought.**
   **A dependent clause does not express a complete thought.**

5.  A.  _____    Although he is determined to win.

   B.  _____    We sent a baby gift basket to our friends.

**SENTENCE COMBINING:**

6.  Zane Gray was an American writer.
    He wrote mostly about the West.

   _____

   _____

**DAY 74**

**CAPITALIZATION:**

1. did grandfather mellon watch <u>leave it to beaver</u> on television when he was young?

**PUNCTUATION:**

2. Is that four poster bed from the movie set of Gone with the Wind

**SUBJECT/VERB:**

**Cross out any prepositional phrases. Underline the subject once and the verb or verb phrase twice:**

3. The banker in the blue suit may have spoken to my grandmother's club.

**PARTS OF SPEECH:   VERBS**

**Write <u>present</u>, <u>past</u>, or <u>future</u> in the space provided:**

4. A. _____ A mason leaves early in the morning.

   B. _____ I shall leave at noon.

   C. _____ A nail technician left her polish on the counter.

**SPELLING:**

**Write the correct spelling of these words:**

5. A. leisure + ly - _____

   B. rip + ed - _____

   C. glory + ous - _____

**SENTENCE COMBINING:**

6. The father whistled loudly.
   The father was impatient.
   The father tried to get his son's attention.

   _____

   _____

**CAPITALIZATION:**

1.  the protestant group meets with rabbi greene to discuss community problems.

**PUNCTUATION:**

2.  A garter snake he believes isnt very scary

**PARTS OF SPEECH:    PRONOUNS**

   **Circle the correct pronoun:**

3.  The Martins and ( they, them ) will be attending a concert together.

**PARTS OF SPEECH:    VERBS**

   **Circle the verb that agrees with the subject:**

4.    A.  The dogs ( like, likes ) the new cushion.
      B.  One of the cats ( meow, meows ) constantly.

**CLAUSES:**

   **Write <u>DC</u> if the clause is dependent; write <u>IC</u> if the clause is independent:**

5.  A.  _____    Tammy didn't sleep well last night.

    B.  _____    Before we dig holes for the fence posts.

**SENTENCE COMBINING:**

6.  Charles Peale painted a portrait of George Washington.
    Charles Peale painted a portrait of Thomas Jefferson.
    Charles Peale painted a portrait of Alexander Hamilton.
    Charles Peale painted a portrait of John Adams.

    _____

    _____

**DAY 76**

**CAPITALIZATION:**

1.   during the space age, neil armstrong walked on the moon.

**PUNCTUATION:**
  **Punctuate the following:**

2.   A.   (magazine)   Seas and Seashells          C.   (story)   The Necklace

     B.   (magazine article)   West Indies Map      D.   (play)   Herbie Rides Again

**PARTS OF SPEECH:    ADVERBS**

3.   Don't give me ( no, any ) excuse.

**PREFIXES/ROOTS/SUFFIXES:**
  **The prefixes uni and mono mean one.**
  **The prefixes du and bi mean two.**
  **The prefix tri means three.**

4.   A.   What is the root of monorail?  _____

     B.   What is a monorail?  _____

     C.   What is the root of a tricycle?  _____

     D.   How many people sing a duet?  _____

**SPELLING:**

  **Write the correct spelling of these words:**

5.   A.   remove + al - _____

     B.   satisfy + ed - _____

     C.   satisfy + ing - _____

**SENTENCE COMBINING:**

6.   A young woman stepped off the train.
     The train was filled with tourists.
     She twisted her ankle.

     _____

     _____

**CAPITALIZATION:**

1.  due to bronchitis, grandpa couldn't work at renicki plumbing last week.

**PUNCTUATION:**

2.  A recipe for creamy spiced sauce was written in Food and Fashion*

*title of a magazine

**PARTS OF SPEECH:    VERBS**

**Write the contraction:**

3.  A.  you will - _____      D.  I am - _____

    B.  where is - _____      E.  have not - _____

    C.  do not - _____      F.  I would - _____

**SENTENCE TYPES:**

**Write the sentence type:**

4.  A.  _____  Is Mary your sister's friend?

    B.  _____  Whoa!  I can't keep up with you!

    C.  _____  Sit here a moment.

**ANALOGIES:**

**Circle the answer that best completes the analogy:**

5.  candle : wick :: forest : _____
    (a) meadow      (b) tree      (c) forester      (d) woods

**SENTENCE COMBINING:**

6.  You must take a number at that deli.
    You will not be served without a number.

    _____

    _____

**DAY 78**

**CAPITALIZATION:**

1.  spencer tracey received an academy award for his acting in <u>captain courageous</u>.

**PUNCTUATION:**

2.

11260 N 58<sup>th</sup> Ave
Glendale AZ   85306
Feb 1  20--

    Dear Koko

        Youre one of my favorite cousins  Lets go to the zoo next week

        Love

        Chandra

**PARTS OF SPEECH:    PRONOUNS**
  **Circle the correct pronoun:**

3.  The person who knows me best is ( he, him ).

**DIRECT OBJECTS:**
  **Cross out any prepositional phrases.  Underline the subject once and the verb or verb phrase twice.  Label any direct objects – <u>D.O.</u>:**

4.  The little boy cuddled a puppy in his arms.

**SPELLING:**
  **Words of two or more syllables that end in consonant + vowel + consonant (CVC) usually do not double the final consonant when adding a suffix.**
        Example:  listen + ing = listening    administer + ed = administered

  **Write the correct spelling of these words:**

5.  A.  allow + ed - _____

    B.  marker + s - _____

    C.  current + ly - _____

**SENTENCE COMBINING:**

6.  The pineal gland is the size of a pea.
    The pineal gland is located at the base of the brain.

    _____

    _____

**CAPITALIZATION:**

1.  a travel agent at trend travel told me about queen victoria's visit to ireland in 1888.

**PUNCTUATION:**

2.  My neighbor likes to watch Jeopardy* and to read short romantic novels
*name of a television show

**PARTS OF SPEECH:     NOUNS**
   **Write the plural:**

3.  A.  foot - _____     D.  proof - _____
    B.  buzz - _____     E.  secretary - _____
    C.  alley - _____     F.  plea - _____

**PARTS OF SPEECH:   ADJECTIVES/ADVERBS**
   **Circle the correct word:**

4.  His partner makes decisions ( slow, slowly ).

**ANALOGIES:**
   **Circle the answer that best completes the analogy:**

5.  trim : prune :: look : _____
    (a) resolve     (b) reciprocate     (c) neglect     (d) scrutinize

**SENTENCE COMBINING:**

6.  Lisa's grandpa can't attend her game.
    Lisa is playing softball.
    Lisa's grandpa has to work.

    _____

    _____

**DAY 80**

**CAPITALIZATION:**

1.  the u. s. marine silent drill team performed at arlington national cemetery.

**PUNCTUATION:**

Punctuate this inside address and salutation of a business letter:

2.  Cardon Co
    2742 E Lewis Street
    Kansas City MO   64111

    Dear Sir

**PARTS OF SPEECH:   VERBS**

Circle any helping verbs; underline the verb phrase twice:

3.  A.  Shirley may be going to Peru soon.

    B.  You could have gone sooner.

    C.  Mr. Keyser has not yet made a decision.

**PARTS OF SPEECH:   ADJECTIVES**
Circle any descriptive adjectives:

4.   A crystal vase held silky pink roses and glass marbles.

**SPELLING:**
Write the correct spelling of these words:

5.  A.  globe + al - _____

    B.  pore + ous - _____

    C.  crazy + ly - _____

**SENTENCE COMBINING:**

6.  Marco is a mechanic.
    He works at Euro Car Repair.
    He works on foreign cars.

    _____

    _____

**CAPITALIZATION:**

1. mt. olympus is near sol duc hot springs in washington.

**PUNCTUATION:**

2. Sharon my cousin lives in Kosciusko Mississippi

**PARTS OF SPEECH:    PRONOUNS**
   **Circle the correct pronouns:**

3. Give ( we, us ) your answer.

**DICTIONARY:    ALPHABETIZING**
   **Place these words in alphabetical order:** rust, lips, lipid, light, rustler, less

4. (a) _____      (d) _____

   (b) _____      (e) _____

   (c) _____      (f) _____

**SENTENCES:**
   **Place a ✓ if the clause is dependent:**

5. A. _____ When the line was drawn.

   B. _____ Jacob finished his art project early.

   C. _____ Which she earned.

**SENTENCE COMBINING:**

6. Mario has had a tonsillectomy.
   Mario is in the hospital.
   The name of the hospital is St. Andrew's Hospital.

   _____

   _____

**DAY 82**

**CAPITALIZATION:**

1.  today's city of casper, wyoming, was once a place on the oregon trail and a pony express stop.

**PUNCTUATION:**

2.  Mrs Schwartz may I read this article entitled Minnesota Draws Tourists for my cur rent events paper

**PARTS OF SPEECH: VERBS**
  **A regular verb adds ed to form both the past and past participle.**

|  | past | past participle |
|---|---|---|
| Example: to gulp: | gulped | (has, have, had) gulped |

  **An irregular verb does not form the past or past participle by adding ed.**
    Example: to sing: sang          (has, have, had) sung

  **Write RV if the verb is regular; write IV if the verb is irregular:**

3.  A. ____ to foam      C. ____ to think      E. ____ to put

    B. ____ to waste     D. ____ to spend     F. ____ to crush

**SUBJECT/VERB:**
  **Cross out any prepositional phrases. Underline the subject once and the verb or verb phrase twice.**

4.  The fans in the first row and the ushers applauded loudly.

**ANALOGIES:**

  **Circle the answer that best completes the analogy:**

5.  plot : scheme :: vow : _____
    (a) marriage      (b) reunion      (c) pledge      (d) priest

**SENTENCE COMBINING:**

6.  Will is sixteen years old.
    He is nearly as tall as his father.

    _____

    _____

## CAPITALIZATION:

### Capitalize these titles:

1. A. "sand dunes"
   B. "incident of the french camp"
   C. "my life with the big cats"

## PUNCTUATION:

2. When youre upset its a good idea to count to ten Wendy

## PARTS OF SPEECH:    VERBS

### Underline the subject once and the verb or verb phrase twice:

3. Stay here.

## PARTS OF SPEECH:    ADJECTIVES

### Circle the correct form:

4. This tie is ( more colorful, most colorful ) than that one.

## SENTENCES:

### Write DC if the clause is dependent; write IC if the clause is independent:

5. A. _____    We stood in line to purchase tickets.
   B. _____    That Dakota left in his back pack.

## SENTENCE COMBINING:

6. The tablecloth is lace.
   It is white.
   It has red rosebuds on it.
   It was crocheted by Pia's mother.

   _____

   _____

**DAY 84**

**CAPITALIZATION:**
**Capitalize this heading, greeting, closing, and signature of a friendly letter:**

1.                                                                     555  maple lane
                                                                       hanover, nj   07936
                                                                       august 1, 2001

    dear lani,                                      sincerely,
                                                                       mary

**PUNCTUATION:**

2.   Dont we need the following lettuce tomatoes and cucumbers

**PARTS OF SPEECH:**

**Circle the correct pronoun:**

3.   ( We, Us ) passengers without children waited to board.

**DICTIONARY:    GUIDE WORDS**

**Guide Words              flag          flew**

**Write Yes if the word will appear on a page with *flag* and flew as guide words.
Write No if the word will not appear on that page.**

4.   A. ____   fast        C. ____   flaw        E. ____   flat
     B. ____   float       D. ____   flue        F. ____   fleet

**ANALOGIES:**

**Circle the answer that best completes the analogy:**

5.   razor : shaving :: sledgehammer : _____
     (a) cutting      (b) tooling      (c) pounding        (d) welding

**SENTENCE COMBINING:**

6.   The couple bought a cottage.
     The cottage is covered with vines.
     It is on a lake.

     _____

     _____

**CAPITALIZATION:**

1.  the television show, <u>fantasy island</u>, made wailua falls in hawaii famous.

**PUNCTUATION:**

2.  The babies diapers arent paper theyre cloth

**PARTS OF SPEECH:    INTERJECTIONS**
   **Write a sentence containing an interjection; circle the interjection:**

3.  _____

**PHRASES/CLAUSES:**
   **Write <u>P</u> if the group of words is a phrase; write <u>C</u> if the group of words is a clause:**

4.  A. _____   Walked to the end of the road.   C. _____   Nicki snickered softly.

   B. _____   Tattered and soiled.   D. _____   Go to the end of the line.

**SPELLING:**
   **Remember:  Words ending in consonant + consonant + <u>e</u> (CCe) usually drop the <u>e</u>**
   **when adding a suffix beginning with a vowel.**
   Example:  dance + ing = dancing    cuddle + ed = cuddled

   **Write the correct spelling of these words:**

5.  A.  belittle + ing - _____

   B.  fray + ed - _____

   C.  dry + ness - _____

**SENTENCE COMBINING:**

6.  Joshua lifted his niece.
   Joshua kissed her.
   Joshua placed her in a highchair.

   _____

   _____

**DAY 86**

**CAPITALIZATION:**

1. is the harvard center for risk analysis working with the u. s. d. a., senator togas?

**PUNCTUATION:**

2. Hurrah  One half of the players on our team will be stars

**PARTS OF SPEECH:    NOUNS/ADJECTIVES**
Write <u>A</u> if the boldfaced word serves as an adjective; write <u>N</u> if the boldfaced word serves as a noun:

3. A. _____    A **golf** club is in his trunk.

   B. _____    Dan likes the game of **golf**.

**PARTS OF SPEECH:    NOUNS**

Circle any nouns:

4. Dad and I often take a bus to town.

**ANALOGIES:**

Circle the answer that best completes the analogy:

5. barely : scarcely :: drowsily : _____
   (a) reluctantly    (b) sleepily    (c) hesitantly    (d) fast

**SENTENCE COMBINING:**

6. Alec is a detective.
   Alec works for the Mirage Police Department.
   Alec enjoys his work.

   _____

   _____

**CAPITALIZATION:**

1.   cole said, "julio and i shopped at woodrow mall near interstate 280 in toledo."

**PUNCTUATION:**

2.   His companys president flew on the Concartia*

*name of an airplane

**LIBRARY:**

3.   Is a biography a fiction or a nonfiction book? _____

**ANTONYMS/HOMONYMS/SYNONYMS:**

4.   A.  An antonym for *genuine* is _____.

    B.  A homonym for *threw* is _____.

    C.  A synonym for *genuine* is _____.

**SENTENCES/FRAGMENTS/RUN-ONS:**

  **Write <u>S</u> for sentence; write <u>F</u> for fragment:**

5.   A.  ____   His arm in a sling.

    B.  ____   Dazed for a few moments.

**SENTENCE COMBINING:**

6.   Neil made scrambled eggs.
    He also made French toast.
    He also made cherry fritters.
    He made this for lunch.

_____

_____

**DAY 88**

**CAPITALIZATION:**

1.   we drove on natchez trace parkway which originally was a native american trail.

**PUNCTUATION:**
   **Punctuate the following:**

2.  A.  (album)   Four Seasons           D.  (story)   The Apprentice

    B.  (song)   In the Garden           E.  (television show)   Parents

    C.  (nursery rhyme)   Little Miss Muffet    F.  (play)   Comedy in Como

**PARTS OF SPEECH:    CONJUNCTIONS**
   **Circle any conjunctions:**

3.   You and I need to leave now, or we may be in trouble.

**PARTS OF SPEECH:    NOUNS**
   **Write a proper noun for each common noun:**

4.   A.  river - _____       C.  team - _____

     B.  person - _____       D.  store - _____

**ANALOGIES:**
   **Circle the answer that best completes the analogy:**

5.   bleak : depressing :: clear : _____
     (a)  vague     (b)  transparent     (c)  opaque     (d)  grotesque

**SENTENCE COMBINING:**

6.   The teenagers watched a movie.
     It was funny.
     They laughed.

     _____

     _____

**CAPITALIZATION:**

1.  his father said, "in 1999, the u. s. lighthouse society helped to revise a list of light stations."

**PUNCTUATION:**

2.  A sun bleached artificial plant was discarded

**PARTS OF SPEECH:   PREPOSITIONS**
    **Circle any prepositions:**

3.  least   perhaps   below   down   for   into   here   until   from

    within   throughout   across   soon   by   again   need   except   his

**PARTS OF SPEECH:   NOUNS**
    **Write the possessive form:**

4.  A.  a notebook belonging to Mrs. James - _____

    B.  a company belonging to two women - _____

    C.  blocks shared by Aaron and Victor - _____

**SPELLING:**
    **Write the correct spelling of these words:**

5.  A.  beauty + ful - _____

    B.  carry + er - _____

    C.  bag + age - _____

**SENTENCE COMBINING:**

6.  Maria watched a basketball game on television.
    It was a championship game.
    She went to the library after that.

    _____

    _____

**DAY 90**

**CAPITALIZATION:**

1.  the mill mountain zoo presented a groundhog day celebration.

**PUNCTUATION:**

**Write the abbreviations for the days of the week:**

2.  A. Sunday - _____      D. Wednesday - _____      G. Saturday - _____

    B. Monday - _____      E. Thursday - _____

    C. Tuesday - _____      F. Friday - _____

**SENTENCES/FRAGMENTS:**
**Write <u>S</u> for sentence; write <u>F</u> for fragment:**

3.  A. _____  In the middle of the street.

    B. _____  Joe with me after the game.

    C. _____  Stones were scattered around.

**PARTS OF SPEECH:   ADJECTIVES**

4.  The three articles that are determining adjectives are _____, _____, and _____.

**SPELLING:**

**Write the correct spelling of these words:**

5.  A. shun + ed - _____

    B. cantor + ing - _____

    C. sloppy + ness - _____

**SENTENCE COMBINING:**

6.  McKinley National Park is in Alaska.
    It was renamed in 1980.
    It was renamed Denali National Park.

    _____

    _____

**CAPITALIZATION:**

1.  grammy kuykendall watched rebox* news while she made dutch apple pies.

*a news network


**PUNCTUATION:**
**Punctuate this outline:**

2.  I  Artists
      A  Impressionistic artists
         1  American
         2  European
            a  Manet
            b  Renoir
      B  Surrealistic artists


**PARTS OF SPEECH:  VERBS**
**Write A if the verb is action; write L if the verb is linking:**

3.  A.  ____  The elderly painter <u>seemed</u> happy in his work.

    B.  ____  The clouds <u>rolled</u> in slowly.


**PARTS OF SPEECH:  ADJECTIVES**
**Circle the predicate adjective in the following sentence:**

4.  His new roller blades were black with purple laces.


**CLAUSES:**
**Write DC if the clause is dependent; write IC if the clause is independent:**
**Remember:   A clause contains a subject and a verb.**
**An independent  clause expresses a complete thought.**
**A dependent clause does not express a complete thought.**

5.  A.  ____  His laughter could be heard downstairs.

    B.  ____  When she bought baseball cards


**SENTENCE COMBINING:**

6.  Idaho is bordered by six Western states.
    Idaho is bordered by a Canadian province.
    The name of the Canadian province is British Columbia.

_____

_____

**DAY 92**

**CAPITALIZATION:**

1. the electives at their junior high include modern dance, german, and cooking 101.

**PUNCTUATION:**
Write the abbreviations for the months. If there is no abbreviation, write the name of the month:

2. A. January- _____    E. May- _____    I. September - _____
   B. February- _____    F. June- _____    J. October - _____
   C. March- _____    G. July- _____    K. November - _____
   D. April - _____    H. August - _____    L. December - _____

**PARTS OF SPEECH:    ADJECTIVES/PRONOUNS**
Sometimes indefinite words serve as adjectives.
Some indefinites are *no, any, some, few, several,* and *many.*
            Example:   Please don't give me **any** spinach.   (adjective modifying *spinach*)

Sometimes an indefinite word stands alone. The indefinite, then, serves as a pronoun.
            Example:   I don't want **any**.   (pronoun)

Write <u>A</u> if the indefinite serves as an adjective; write <u>P</u> if it serves as a pronoun:

3. A. _____    **Several** dollars fell from his wallet.
   B. _____    **Several** will receive prizes.

**PARTS OF SPEECH:    VERBS**

4. *To + verb* is called a/an _____.

**ANALOGIES:**

Circle the answer that best completes the analogy:

5. imply : insinuate :: abduct : _____
   (a) calculate      (b) reduce      (c) kidnap      (d) arrange

**SENTENCE COMBINING:**

6. Labor Day is a holiday in the United States.
   Labor Day is a holiday in Canada.
   It honors the laborer.

   _____

   _____

**CAPITALIZATION:**
   **Capitalize these titles:**

1.  A.   "beautiful dreamer"

    B.   staking her claim

    C.   "how do i love thee"

**PUNCTUATION:**
   **Punctuate this inside address and salutation of a business letter:**

2.   Japanese Flower Co
     456 N Ukiah Pl
     Kokomo IN   46902

     Dear Mr Yakimoto

**DIFFICULT WORDS:**
   **Circle the correct word:**

3.  A.  ( There, Their, They're ) running late.
    B.  ( Your, You're ) face is dirty.
    C.  He (don't, doesn't ) know how to do it.

**PARTS OF SPEECH:     NOUNS**
   **Circle any proper noun:**

4.   Sir Francis Drake, an Englishman, sailed into San Francisco Bay.

**ANALOGIES:**
   **Circle the answer that best completes the analogy:**

5.   ailing : thriving :: concealed : _____
     (a) reliable     (b) hidden       (c) harsh        (d) exposed

**SENTENCE COMBINING:**

6.   The sack is made of velvet.
     It contains several gold coins.
     Ramona found the sack in an old chest.

     _____

     _____

**DAY 94**

**CAPITALIZATION:**

1.  in the spring, the ross family will visit palomar college in california.

**PUNCTUATION:**

**Punctuate this greeting, body, and closing of a friendly letter:**

2.  Dear Alice
    Mindys father in law was born in Alabaster Alabama on September 23 1952
    Will this information help you to write your business report
                                                        Always
                                                        Dean

**PARTS OF SPEECH:    NOUNS**

3.  Words ending in ____, ____, ____, _____, and ____ add *es* to form the plural.

**PARTS OF SPEECH:    ADVERBS**

**Write the comparative form of *well*:**

4.  The hotel maid cleaned the room _____ on Monday than on Tuesday.

**SPELLING:**

**Write the correct spelling of the following words:**

5.  A.  reprimand + ing - _____

    B.  century + s - _____

    C.  response + ive - _____

**SENTENCE COMBINING:**

6.  The Pyrenees Mountains separate Spain from France.
    The Pyrenees Mountains are rich in timber.

    _____

    _____

**CAPITALIZATION:**

1. the atlantic ocean and the mediterranean sea border the continent of africa.

**PUNCTUATION:**
   **Place a dash (the width of M) or parentheses (  ) to provide additional information.**
       Example:   I never understood his reasoning – until now.
                  I never understood his reasoning (until now).

2. The group held a meeting in Dallas Texas last winter  odd time for golfers

**PARTS OF SPEECH:    VERBS**
   **The perfect tense is made up of a form of to have + a past participle.**
       **For the present perfect, *has* or *have* is used. (The verb must agree with the subject.)**
       **For the past perfect, *had* is used.**
       **For the future perfect, *shall have* or *will have* is used.**
             Example:   past perfect of *to ride* =   had ridden
   **Write the tense:**

3.  A.  _____  present perfect of *to go*
    B.  _____  past perfect of *to go*

**SUBJECT/VERB**

   **Underline the subject once and the verb or verb phrase twice:**

4. Haven't you finished the ironing?

**ANALOGIES:**
   **Analogies can show a variety of relationships.  Always determine how the
   first two words of a set are related; then, choose the answer that best reflects
   that same relationship with the third word.**
   **Circle the answer that best completes the analogy:**

5. Paris : France :: London : _____
   (a) city      (b) England      (c) Europe      (d) Buckingham Palace

**SENTENCE COMBINING:**

6. These are chairs for the patio.
   Susie bought them at Today's Outdoor Store.
   They are called Adirondack chairs.

   _____

   _____

**DAY 96**

**CAPITALIZATION:**

1.   rare orangutans roam in the sepilok sanctuary on the island of borneo.

**PUNCTUATION:**

2.   These four may go  Dawn Christy Jacob and Tate

**PARTS OF SPEECH:    NOUNS**

3.   What kind of noun is *fear*?  _____

**PARTS OF SPEECH:    PRONOUNS**

   **Write the antecedent for the boldfaced pronoun:**

4.   The large gray cat carried **its** kittens to a new place.

**SPELLING:**

   **Write the correct spelling of the following words:**

5.   A.   startle + ing - _____

      B.   strap + ed - _____

      C.   insure + ance - _____

**SENTENCE COMBINING:**

6.   The man placed a ring on a plate.
      The ring was an engagement ring.
      The plate was a dessert plate.
      He smiled.

      _____

      _____

**CAPITALIZATION:**

1. his son who has an upper respiratory infection went to dogwood medical clinic in georgia.

**PUNCTUATION:**

2. Their teams final score was twenty seven points  said Cole

**PARTS OF SPEECH:    NOUNS**

   **Circle the predicate nominative:**

3. Martha's aunt became a lawyer in Atlanta, Georgia.

**PHRASES/CLAUSES:**

   **Write P if the group of words is a phrase; write C if the group of words is a clause:**

4. A. _____    Following the white cement truck.

    B. _____    Followed by a white cement truck.

    C. _____    A mailman was following a white cement truck.

**ANALOGIES:**
   **Circle the answer that best completes the analogy:**

5. city : Minneapolis :: landmark : _____
    (a) South Dakota      (b) ruins      (c) Washington Monument      (d) Austin

**SENTENCE COMBINING:**

6. The Women's Army Corp was formed in 1942.
   It was established after the United States entered World War II.

   _____

   _____

**DAY 98**

**CAPITALIZATION:**
   **Capitalize these titles:**

1.  A.  (story)   "girl with a dream"

    B.  (book)   <u>the night they burned the mountain</u>

    C.  (poem)   "an old woman of the roads"


**PUNCTUATION:**

2.  Eli said  Go east on Bear Blvd until you come to a Y shaped street


**LIBRARY:**

3.  A _____ dictionary gives names of places such as cities (Racine),
    water forms (Niagara Falls), and landforms (Manihiki Island).  It supplies information about
    these places.


**PARTS OF SPEECH:    PRONOUNS**
   **Circle the correct pronoun:**

4.  Becky has read more books than ( I, me ).


**SPELLING:**
   **Words ending in consonant + e usually drop the e when adding a suffix
   beginning with a vowel.  However, when that final consonant is c or g, the
   e is not usually dropped when adding the suffix, able.**
       Examples:   love + able = lovable   recharge + able = rechargeable

   **Write the correct spelling of these words:**

5.  A.  debate + able - _____

    B.  change + able - _____

    C.  erase + able - _____


**SENTENCE COMBINING:**

6.  His pants are covered with paint.
    They are his favorite pants.
    He continues to wear them.

    _____

    _____

**CAPITALIZATION:**

1.   on november 11, an armistice day parade honored those in world war II.


**PUNCTUATION:**
   **Punctuate the following:**

2.   A.   (newspaper)   Valley Independent          C.   (painting)   Eleanor

   B.   (newspaper article)   Celebrations          D.   (poem)   A Dutch Picture


**ALPHABETIZING:**
   **Write these words in alphabetical order:**   knack, idea, jest, koala, know, jeep

3.   (a) _____          (d) _____

   (b) _____          (e) _____

   (c) _____          (f) _____


**PARTS OF SPEECH:     ADJECTIVES**
   **Write <u>A</u> if the boldfaced word serves as an adjective; write <u>N</u> if the boldfaced word serves as a noun:**

4.   A.   _____          **Strawberry** ice cream is his favorite.
   B.   _____          The farmer pulled a **strawberry** from a plant.
   C.   _____          **Computer** paper was ordered.
   D.   _____          Margaret is learning to use a **computer** at her office.


**CLAUSES:**
   **Write <u>DC</u> if the clause is dependent; write <u>IC</u> if the clause is independent:**

5.   A.   _____          Deka is an accountant for a major firm.
   B.   _____          Unless Mario buys more stock.


**SENTENCE COMBINING:**

6.   They needed sheets for a king-size bed.
     They bought sheets for a queen-size bed.

     _____

     _____

**DAY 100**

**CAPITALIZATION:**

1. the himalaya mountains lie in southern asia and border india.

**PUNCTUATION:**

2. A tall handsome cowboy a rodeo star left for Billings Montana

**PARTS OF SPEECH:**
   **Write the contraction:**

3. A. she is - _____   D. did not - _____   G. has not - _____

   B. we are - _____   E. they will - _____   H. will not - _____

   C. cannot - _____   F. should not - _____   I. I have - _____

**SENTENCE TYPES:**
   **Write the type of sentence:**

4. A. _____ Come here.

   B. _____ It's hot!

   C. _____ This drawer is stuck again.

   D. _____ Will you finish this for us?

**CLAUSES:**
   **Write DC if the clause is dependent; write IC if the clause is independent:**

5. A. _____ Mrs. Childs corrected her error.

   B. _____ That John gave me for my birthday.

**SENTENCE COMBINING:**

6. Cos lettuce is also called romaine lettuce.
   It can withstand heat better than other lettuces.

   _____

   _____

**CAPITALIZATION:**

1. we visited hosewell plantation, the birthplace of thomas lynch, jr., who signed the declaration of independence.

**PUNCTUATION:**

2. On Tuesday July 3 1992 we went camping in Bangor Maine

**PARTS OF SPEECH:**
**Underline the entire verb phrase:**

3. A. He must have ( brought, brung ) this brochure.
   B. Should I have ( taken, took ) this brochure?
   C. Mr. Scott may not have ( went, gone ).
   D. Jay had ( drank, drunk ) all the milk.

**PARTS OF SPEECH:    ADVERBS**
**Circle any adverbs:**

4. Later, we must look everywhere for a rather unusual gift.

**ANALOGIES:**
**Circle the answer that best completes the analogy:**

5. shortage : abundance :: deceit : _____
   (a) swindle     (b) fraud     (c) trickery     (d) honesty

**SENTENCE COMBINING:**

6. The child refused to cooperate.
   The child sat on a chair.
   The child pouted.

   _____

   _____

**DAY 102**

**CAPITALIZATION:**

1.  miss arter, a canadian teacher at logan junior high school, also speaks basque.

**PUNCTUATION:**

2.  Her address is 245 Linx Lane Espanola New Mexico   87532

**PARTS OF SPEECH:     VERBS**

The perfect tense is made up of a form of <u>to have</u> + a past participle.
For the present perfect, *has* or *have* is used. (The verb must agree with the subject.)
For the past perfect, *had* is used.
For the future perfect, *shall have* or *will have* is used.
Example:   present perfect of *to swim*  =   <u>has swum or have swum</u>

**Write the tense:**

3.  A.  _____  past perfect of *to break*

B.  _____  future perfect of *to speak*

**PARTS OF SPEECH:     ADJECTIVES**

**Circle any adjectives**:

4.  Five small, shaggy spaniels romped across the green Irish countryside.

**SENTENCES:**

**Place a ✔ if the clause is dependent:**

5.  A.  _____  When the line was drawn.

B.  _____  Jacob finished his art project early.

C.  _____  Which she earned.

**SENTENCE COMBINING:**

6.  Macadamia nuts are native to Australia.
They are also found in Hawaii.

_____

_____

**CAPITALIZATION:**

1. stephen foster wrote the song, "my old kentucky home," in bardstown, kentucky.

**PUNCTUATION:**
   **Place a dash (the width of <u>M</u>) or parentheses ( ) to provide additional information.**
      Examples:  The waiters – Todd, Chan, and Bo – are here.
         *Using commas for an appositive in this sentence would result in to*
         *many commas.  It is better to separate the phrase with dashes.*

      I demanded (in a nice tone of voice) that he give me his book.

2. If you arent ready well wait  for five minutes

**PARTS OF SPEECH:    VERBS**

   **Select the verb that agrees with the subject:**

3. Each of the tennis players ( serve, serves ) extremely well.

**ANTONYMS/HOMONYMS/SYNONYMS:**

4.  A.  An antonym for *courteous* is _____.

    B.  A homonym for *rain* is _____.

    C.  A synonym for *friend* is _____.

**ANALOGIES:**

   **Circle the answer that best completes the analogy:**

5. nail : cuticle :: camera  : _____
   (a) photography     (b) lens   (c) tripod     (d) picture

**SENTENCE COMBINING:**

6. Vinnie has been transferred to Olympia.
   He is looking forward to it.
   He has never been to Olympia.

   _____

   _____

**DAY 104**

**CAPITALIZATION:**

1. "the populist party was formed to express american farmers' opinions," mia said.


**PUNCTUATION:**

2. After Lauras essay entitled Famous Women was read everyone applauded


**PARTS OF SPEECH:    ADJECTIVES/ADVERBS**

   **Select the correct word:**

3. Micah and Anthony are great players.

   They play _____ ( good, well) together.


**DIRECT OBJECTS:**

   **Cross out any prepositional phrases.  Underline the subject once and the verb
   or verb phrase twice.  Label any direct object – <u>D.O.</u>**

4. During the early morning, the girls had ridden horses for two hours.


**SIMPLE AND COMPOUND SENTENCES:**
   **A simple sentence has a subject and verb *and* expresses a complete thought.**
             Example:    During the evening hours, those <u>birds</u> usually <u>gather</u> in our trees.

   **A compound sentence contains two (or more) independent clauses (complete thoughts).**
             Example:    Koko planted a flower garden, but she didn't water it.
                              *independent clause*              *independent clause*
   **Write <u>S</u> if the sentence is simple; write <u>C</u> if the sentence is compound:**

5. A. _____    Jemima likes to water-ski.
   B. _____    Derek nodded and grabbed his kite.
   C. _____    You must hurry, or we'll be late.


**SENTENCE COMBINING:**

6. A hammerhead is a type of shark.
   A hammerhead is also an African bird.

   _____

   _____

**CAPITALIZATION:**

1. did lieutenant zebulon pike of the u. s. army lead an expedition to spanish new mexico?

**PUNCTUATION:**

2. On April 14 2001 I listened to the Presidents remarks   said Brian

**PARTS OF SPEECH:   PREPOSITIONS**
  **Cross out any prepositional phrases.  Underline the subject once and the verb or verb phrase twice:**

3. Across the street and past the old mill lives a ranger with his wife and dog.

**DICTIONARY:   ALPHABETIZING**
 **Write these words in alphabetical order:**  order, limousine, minister, limb, orator, misery

4.  (a) _____        (d) _____

    (b) _____        (e) _____

    (c) _____        (f) _____

**SPELLING:**

  **Write the correct spelling of these words:**

5.  A.  tire + some - _____

    B.  salvage + able - _____

    C.  contour + ing - _____

**SENTENCE COMBINING:**

6.  All of the campsites were taken.
    The camping area was closed.
    The camping area is by a stream.

    _____

    _____

**DAY 106**

**CAPITALIZATION:**

1. the shen yang zoo houses a siberian tiger, one of the world's endangered species.

**PUNCTUATION:**

2. Read Witter Bynners poem entitled A Farmer Remembers Lincoln if you have time

**PREFIXES/ROOTS/SUFFIXES:**

The prefixes il, im, in, ir, non, and un means *not*.

Write a word beginning with one of the prefixes meaning *not*:

3. A. not possible - _____    D. not common - _____

   B. not legal - _____    E. not toxic - _____

   C. not valid - _____    F. not responsible - _____

**PARTS OF SPEECH:    ADVERBS**

Write the correct form:

4. A. He did the carving _____ ( comparative of carefully ) than I.

   B. Of the four men, my dad sings _____ ( superlative of well ).

**SIMPLE/COMPOUND SENTENCES:**

Write a simple sentence with a compound verb:

5. _____

   _____

**SENTENCE COMBINING:**

6. The traveler was taking a picture.
   It was of a plantation.
   He was in the South.
   He fell backwards at the same time.

   _____

   _____

**CAPITALIZATION:**

1.  in 1707, the act of union created great britain by joining england and scotland.

**PUNCTUATION:**

2.  Our ladies club gave twenty one scholarships to seniors  said the president

**PARTS OF SPEECH:    ADJECTIVES**
   **Write the correct form:**

3.  A.  My tablet paper is _____ ( comparative of heavy ) than waxed paper.

   B.  In their family, Douglas is the _____ ( superlative of good ) bowler.

**LIBRARY:**

4.  A _____ is a book that gives synonyms.

**SENTENCES:**
   **Write DC if the clause is dependent; write IC if the clause is independent:**

5.  A.  _____  Marco has a pinto horse.
   B.  _____  Although his elbow was hurt.

**SENTENCE COMBINING:**

6.  The family is riding a trolley.
    The family is sightseeing.
    The family is visiting San Francisco.

    _____

    _____

**DAY 108**

**CAPITALIZATION:**

1.  the u. s. court of appeals heard a case regarding the united states environmental protection agency.

**PUNCTUATION:**

2.  Rule 1    Pick up paper
    Rule 2    Use trash containers

**PARTS OF SPEECH:    PRONOUNS**

   **Circle the correct pronoun:**

3.  "( Us, We ) teachers need to make a decision," announced Miss Snell.

**PARTS OF SPEECH:    NOUNS**

4.  What type of noun is apartment? _____

**ANALOGIES:**

   **Circle the answer that best completes the analogy:**

5.  tongue : mouth :: anchor : _____
    (a)  weight      (b)  freighter      (c)  ocean      (d)  maritime

**SENTENCE COMBINING:**

6.  The ship docked at Long Beach.
    It was a cruise ship.
    It had just returned from Mexico.

    _____

    _____

**CAPITALIZATION:**

1.  my mother bought italian tile at floor coverings unlimited on fairfield avenue.

**PUNCTUATION:**

**Punctuate these titles:**

2.  A.  (newspaper)   City News

    B.  (essay)   Every Dog Should Own a Man

    C.  (story)   The Long Winter

    D.  (book)   Lassie

**PARTS OF SPEECH:    VERBS**
**Cross out any prepositional phrases.  Underline the subject once and the verb or verb phrase twice:**

3.  A.  Stay in your chair.

    B.  The custodian cleaned the bathroom and vacuumed the hall.

    C.  Neither Gloria nor Zak may go alone.

**SENTENCE/FRAGMENTS:**
**Write S for sentence; write F for fragment:**

4.  A.  _____   Fireworks off in the sky.
    B.  _____   Exploding in the sky.
    C.  _____   Fireworks exploded in the sky.

**PHRASES:**

5.  Write an example of a phrase: _____

**SENTENCE COMBINING:**

6.  Bobby Orr is a hockey player.
    Bobby Orr is the first defenseman to score one hundred points.

    _____

    _____

**DAY 110**

**CAPITALIZATION:**

1.  did dorothea lange take famous pictures of the midwest during the great depression?

**PUNCTUATION:**

2.  Will forty seven books be shipped to Duluth Minnesota  asked Kyle

**FRAGMENTS/SENTENCES/RUN-ONS:**
   **Determine if the group of words is a sentence (<u>S</u>), fragment (<u>F</u>), or run-on (<u>R-O</u>):**

3.  A.  _____  Shouting loudly, he in the back row.
    B.  _____  The heart beat showed irregularities.
    C.  _____  Some pedestrians crossed in the crosswalk others waited on the corner for their friends.

**PARTS OF SPEECH:   VERBS**
   **Write the verb tense:**

4.  A.  _____ ( present tense of *to taste* )
    B.  _____ ( future tense of *to collect* )
    C.  _____ ( past tense of *to grow* )
    D.  _____ ( past tense of *to paint* )

**ANALOGIES:**

   **Circle the answer that best completes the analogy:**

5.  flawless: perfect :: tasteless : _____
    (a) appetizing      (b) tangy      (c) bland      (d) tongue

**SENTENCE COMBINING:**

6.  James Bowie fought at the Alamo.
    James Bowie died at the Alamo.
    The Alamo is in Texas.

    _____

    _____

**CAPITALIZATION:**

1.  she flew to crystal airport located near route 100 in the minneapolis area.

**PUNCTUATION:**

2.  The class of 92 in fact had many honor students  said the commencement speaker

**PARTS OF SPEECH:   ADVERBS**

   **Write the correct word:**

3.  I have never seen ( anybody, nobody ) so protective.

**PARTS OF SPEECH:   NOUNS**

   **Write the plural of the following nouns:**

4.  A.  hope = _____          E.  louse = _____

    B.  life = _____          F.  elk = _____

    C.  dash = _____          G.  mother-in-law = _____

    D.  cyst = _____          H.  tress = _____

**SIMPLE/COMPOUND/COMPLEX SENTENCES:**

   **Finish this compound sentence:**

5.  Janet wants to go to Alaska, but _____

**SENTENCE COMBINING:**

6.  Anne Richards was born in Waco, Texas.
    She became governor of Texas in 1990.

    _____

    _____

**DAY 112**

**CAPITALIZATION:**

1.  mayor yazzie remarked, "the suez canal, i think, is the most important constructed waterway in the eastern hemisphere."

**PUNCTUATION:**

2.  Is those kindergarteners favorite song Itsy Bitsy Spider

**PARTS OF SPEECH:    NOUNS**

**Write <u>P</u> if the word is a proper noun; write <u>C</u> if the word is a common noun:**

3.  A.  ____ OCEAN              D.  ____ TOWER

    B.  ____ ARCTIC OCEAN        E.  ____ SEARS TOWER

    C.  ____ BUILDING            F.  ____ FRIENDS

**WORDS:**

  **Circle the correct word:**

4.  A.  ( There, Their, They're ) opinion was not favorable.

    B.  ( Your, You're ) the first person in the first row.

    C.  ( It's, Its ) fur was covered with briars.

    D.  He ( don't, doesn't ) know where to look.

**SPELLING:**

  **Write the correct spelling of these words:**

5.  A.  healthy + est - _____

    B.  pronounce + able - _____

    D.  evict + ed - _____

**SENTENCE COMBINING:**

6.  Jemima was stung by a bee.
    Jemima wailed loudly.

    _____

    _____

**CAPITALIZATION:**

1.   the treaty that added the louisiana territory to america was approved by congress.

**PUNCTUATION:**

2.   The Star Spangled Banner is our countrys national anthem

**PARTS OF SPEECH:    VERBS**

3.   *To + verb* is called an _____.

**FRIENDLY LETTERS/ENVELOPES:**
   **Write your return address on this envelope:**

4. _____

   _____

   _____

   _____

                                             Mr. and Mrs. H. Mancutti
                                             345 Sydney Place
                                             Plumsteadville, PA  18949

_____

**ANALOGIES:**

   **Circle the answer that best completes the analogy:**

5.   devise : create :: implore : _____
      (a) beg      (b) revolt      (c) discern      (d) denounce

**SENTENCE COMBINING:**

6.   Fog occurs when there is excess moisture in the air.
      The moisture attaches to dust particles.
      The dust particles are microscopic.

   _____

   _____

**DAY 114**

**CAPITALIZATION:**

1. dino and i saw dunton, a ghost town, and went through cinnamon pass in colorado's san juan mountains.

**PUNCTUATION:**

2. The Memphis Bell* left London England at 5 30 in the morning

*name of a plane

**PARTS OF SPEECH:    NOUNS**

**Write the possessive form:**

3. A. a son belonging to Brenda - _____

   B. a house belonging to Sheila and Toby - _____

   C. a dish belonging to three cats - _____

   D. a treasurer of a club - _____

**WORDS:**

**Circle the correct word:**

4. A. ( There, Their, They're ) are two senators from each state.
   B. ( It's, Its ) not too late to enter.
   C. I want to go, ( to, two, too ).

**SPELLING:**

**Write the correct spelling of the following words:**

5. A. remind + er - _____

   B. sincere + ly - _____

   C. mar + ed - _____

   D. tear + ful - _____

**SENTENCE COMBINING:**

6. John Keats was a famous poet in England.
   He almost became a surgeon.

   _____

   _____

**CAPITALIZATION:**

1.  in 1206, genghis kahn founded the mongol empire in china.

**PUNCTUATION:**

2.  Marge have you asked Bridgette watched Puppet Play*

*name of a television show

**PARTS OF SPEECH:    NOUNS**

**Write the possessive form:**

3.  A.  a pet belonging to a farm - _____

    B.  a post card purchased by two tourists - _____

    C.  some shoes belonging to Misty - _____

    D.  some cavities in more than one tooth - _____

**SENTENCE TYPES:**

4.  A.  Write a declarative sentence: _____

    B.  Write an imperative sentence: _____

**ANALOGIES:**

**Circle the answer that best completes the analogy:**

5.  heed : disregard :: significant : _____
    (a) trivial    (b) ornate    (c) relevant    (d) willful

**SENTENCE COMBINING:**

6.  Sarah Jewett was an American.
    She was an author.
    She wrote about life in towns.
    These towns were in New England.

    _____

    _____

**DAY 116**

**CAPITALIZATION:**

1. president william harrison, who had been governor of the indiana territory, died after just one month in office?

**PUNCTUATION:**

**Punctuate the inside address and greeting of this business letter:**

2. Granite Concepts Co Inc
   120 W Conrad Ave
   Betterton  MD   21610

   Dear Mr Carnell

**PARTS OF SPEECH:    VERBS**

3. The present participle of *to laugh* is _____.

**DIRECT OBJECTS/INDIRECT OBJECTS/OBJECTS OF THE PREPOSITION:**

**Using the following sentence, answer the questions:**

*My friend gave her mother a card for her birthday.*

4. A.  The direct object is _____.
   B.  The indirect object is _____.
   C.  The object of the preposition is _____.

**SPELLING:**

**Write the correct spelling of the following words:**

5. A.  navy + s - _____

   B.  buoy + s - _____

**SENTENCE COMBINING:**

6. Dora works at Bandix Bank.
   She is a loan officer.
   The bank is on Jefferson Street.

   _____

   _____

**CAPITALIZATION:**

1.  on new year's eve, they drove around the campus of piedmont technical college.

**PUNCTUATION:**

2.  Marco Polo the great traveler to Asia lived around 1300 A D

**FRIENDLY LETTERS/ENVELOPES:**
Write your return address;  address the envelope to Mr. Charles Glove who lives at 12 Amble Road in Broken Arrow, Oklahoma   74011:

3. _____

   _____

   _____

   _____


   _____

**PREFIXES/ROOTS/SUFFIXES:**
Roots have meanings.          Example:  script = write
Write the meaning of each word; use a dictionary if necessary:

4.  A.  inscription - _____
    B.  scripture - _____
    C.  transcript - _____

**SIMPLE/COMPOUND/COMPLEX SENTENCES:**
Write a compound sentence:

5.  _____

**SENTENCE COMBINING:**

6.  Our picnic has been canceled.
    It was canceled due to rain.
    It has been rescheduled for next week.

    _____

    _____

**DAY 118**

**CAPITALIZATION:**
   **Capitalize this outline:**

1. i.   furniture

   a.   beds

      1.   types of beds

      2.   care of beds

   b.   chairs

   ii.   belongings


**PUNCTUATION:**

2.   She asked Mrs Reed her social studies teacher if Zermatt Switzerland is at the base of the Matterhorn


**PHRASES/CLAUSES:**

   **Select the correct word:**

3.   A _____ ( phrase, clause ) always has a subject and a verb.


**PARTS OF SPEECH:    ADJECTIVES**

   **Circle the predicate adjective in the following sentence:**

4.   Matthew Brady's photographs of Civil War scenes are very valuable.


**ANALOGIES:**

   **Circle the answer that best completes the analogy:**

5.   machine : copier :: storm : _____
     (a) barometer      (b) waves      (c) lull      (d) typhoon


**SENTENCE COMBINING:**

6.   Tessa is making a cradle.
     The cradle is for her friend's new baby.
     Tessa is measuring a piece of wood.

     _____

     _____

**CAPITALIZATION:**

**Capitalize these titles:**

1. A. <u>new hampshire climbing guide</u>

   B. <u>north of cheyenne</u>

   C. "proud on my broken heart"

**PUNCTUATION:**

2. A hummingbird approached the flower but it didnt stay

**PARTS OF SPEECH:   NOUNS**

3. Add <u>es</u> to form the plural for nouns ending in _____, _____, _____, _____, and _____.

**PARTS OF SPEECH:   PRONOUNS**

**Circle the correct answer:**

4. A. ( Clay and I, Me and Clay ) have found a ferret.

   B. Please don't go without my sister and ( I, me ).

   C. These travelers have waited longer than ( we, us ).

**SIMPLE/COMPOUND/COMPLEX SENTENCES:**

**Write <u>S</u> if the sentence is simple; write <u>C</u> if the sentence is compound:**

5. A. _____   His cowboy boots need to be cleaned.

   B. _____   Mona pretended to stumble and grinned at us.

**SENTENCE COMBINING:**

6. Their grandpa works in computers.
   He is a programmer.
   He also volunteers at a health clinic.

   _____

   _____

**DAY 120**

**CAPITALIZATION:**

1.  has corporal rio taken a taxi to horst hotel by price parkway?

**PUNCTUATION:**

2.  When the artists conference meets here theyll need tea coffee and milk for lunch

**PARTS OF SPEECH:    VERBS**

3.  List the 23 helping verbs: _____

    _____

    _____

**PREFIXES/ROOTS/SUFFIXES:**

  **Write the suffix of the following words:**

4.  A.  dangerous - _____        C.  gleeful - _____        E.  careless - _____

    B.  happiness - _____        D.  quietly - _____        F.  diver  - _____

**SPELLING:**

  **Write the correct spelling of these words:**

5.  A.  property + s - _____

    B.  exchange + able - _____

    C.  spin + ing - _____

**SENTENCE COMBINING:**

6.  Lady Jane Grey was the queen of England.
    She was queen for only nine days.
    After that, she was imprisoned.

    _____

    _____

**CAPITALIZATION:**

1.  does tate like the poem entitled "she walks in beauty" by lord byron?

**PUNCTUATION:**

2.  Cars trucks and vans parked along the long tree lined street

**PARTS OF SPEECH:   ADVERBS**

**Circle the correct word:**

3.  A.  The shoe repairman fixed the shoes ( good, well ).
    B.  He ( seldom, seldomly ) rises early.
    C.  Don't walk so ( slow, slowly ).

**PARTS OF SPEECH:   PRONOUNS**

**Select the antecedent(s) for the possessive pronoun:**

4.  The secretary and treasurer must submit their reports by Friday.

**ANALOGIES:**

**Circle the answer that best completes the analogy:**

5.  dog : greyhound :: entertainer : _____
    (a) acrobat    (b) amusement    (c) movie    (d) laughter

**SENTENCE COMBINING:**

6.  Juan ordered a chicken sandwich.
    He wanted it on whole wheat bread.
    He asked for extra mayonnaise.

    _____

    _____

**DAY 122**

**CAPITALIZATION:**

1.  a scene in the 1954 movie, <u>broken arrow</u>, was filmed near chapel of the holy cross.


**PUNCTUATION:**

2.  The Hapton Express* leaves at 4 40 on Monday June 25

*name of a train


**DICTIONARY:   GUIDE WORDS**

Will the following words be found on the dictionary page with the guide words, *thirst* and *threat*?  Write <u>Yes</u> or <u>No</u> in the blank:

3.  A. ____ thirsty          C. ____ theme

    B. ____ thistle          D. ____ three


**PARTS OF SPEECH:   NOUNS**

Write <u>A</u> if the noun is abstract;  write <u>C</u> if the noun is concrete:

4.  A. ____ gravity    C. ____ antelope    E. ____ bacon

    B. ____ honor      D. ____ vitamin     F. ____ graciousness


**ANALOGIES:**

Circle the answer that best completes the analogy:

5.  crispy : soggy :: devious : _____
    (a) mistaken     (b) changeable    (c) deceptive    (d) straightforward


**SENTENCE COMBINING:**

6.  Chopsticks may refer to wooden sticks used for eating.
    Chopsticks may refer to a type of piano tune.

    _____

    _____

**CAPITALIZATION:**

1. did dr. and mrs. wong attend the oakville waterfront festival held in bronte heritage waterfront park, sara?

**PUNCTUATION:**

2. Joyce Davis R N doesnt work at St Lukes Hospital in Phoenix Arizona

**PARTS OF SPEECH:  ADVERBS OR PREPOSITIONS**

Write <u>A</u> in the space provided if the boldfaced word serves as an adverb; write <u>P</u> in the space if the boldfaced word serves as a preposition:

3. A. _____ Let's walk **over** the bridge.
   B. _____ Please come **over** here.
   C. _____ The Puritans came **over** to America after the Pilgrims arrived.

**LIBRARY:**

4. The three types of cards in the card catalog are _____, _____, and _____.

**SPELLING:**

Write the correct spelling of the following words:

5. A. balcony + s - _____

   B. reply + ed - _____

   C. supply + ing - _____

**SENTENCE COMBINING:**

6. A mukluk is an Eskimo boot.
   It may be made of seal skin.
   It may be made of reindeer skin.

   _____

   _____

**DAY 124**

## CAPITALIZATION:
**Capitalize this friendly letter:**

1.
                                        73354 stanley blvd.

                                        east greenwich, ri   02818

                                        november 2, 20—

   dear chuck,

      my new ottenstroer bike is really neat.  we're going riding soon.

                                        your friend,

                                        chan

## PUNCTUATION:

2.   You have too many ts in litttle Fran

## SUBJECT/VERB:
**Underline the subject once and the verb or verb phrase twice:**

3.   A shopper crossed the street and ambled into a clothing store.

## DIFFICULT WORDS:
**Circle the correct word:**

4.   A.   It's not ( there, their, they're ) fault.

     B.   They ( sneaked, snuck ) past us.

     C.   The roller coaster rider was not ( affected, effected ) by the fast motion.

## ANALOGIES:

**Circle the answer that best completes the analogy:**

5.   container : barrel :: physician : _____
     (a) doctor      (b) clinic      (c) assistant        (d) dermatologist

## SENTENCE COMBINING:

6.   Lenny cannot attend the teachers' conference.
     Laura cannot attend the teachers' conference.
     The conference will be held in Baltimore, Maryland.

     _____

     _____

**CAPITALIZATION:**

1.  does the diamonds and denims gala* support the american cancer society?

*name of a celebration

**PUNCTUATION:**

2.  Your lamp the one thats very heavy needs to be shipped in a large sturdy carton

**PARTS OF SPEECH:    ADVERBS**

  **Circle the correct word:**

3.  A.   "I don't have ( none, any )," remarked Millie.

    B.   He hardly has (nothing, anything ) to do.

**ANTONYMS/SYNONYMS/HOMONYMS:**

4.  A.   An antonym for positive is _____.

    B.   A homonym for stationery is _____.

    C.   A synonym for creative is _____.

**SPELLING:**

  **Write the correct spelling of these words:**

5.  A.   scent + ed - _____

    B.   believe + able - _____

    C.   certain + ty - _____

**SENTENCE COMBINING:**

6.  Hemlock is an evergreen tree.
    Poisonous hemlock is an herb.

    _____

    _____

**DAY 126**

**CAPITALIZATION:**

1. "sixth grade students are studying french and american government at lason private school," said representative loster.

**PUNCTUATION:**

2. A secretaries meeting was held last Tues April 12$^{th}$ at 10 30 A M

**ENVELOPE:**

Write your return address on the envelope and address the letter to Mrs. Hope Harmon who lives at 12342 North Lane in Rusk, Texas. The zip code is 75785.

3. _____

   _____     _____

   _____     _____

   _____     _____


   _____

**DICTIONARY:   ALPHABETIZING**

Write these words in alphabetical order:   shanty, shark, shank, shapely, shaggy

4.   _____

**ANALOGIES:**

Circle the answer that best completes the analogy:

5. dependable : responsible :: dangerous : _____
   (a) courageous     (b) hazardous     (c) secure     (d) harmless

**SENTENCE COMBINING:**

6. This silk shirt may be dry-cleaned.
   This rayon shirt must be dry-cleaned.

   _____

   _____

**CAPITALIZATION:**

1. "have you," asked mario, "been to waterpocket canyon in utah?"


**PUNCTUATION:**

2. The building of the Panama Canal began in 1904 however it didnt open until 1914


**PARTS OF SPEECH:    VERBS**

   **Select the correct verb:**

3. Either the parakeet or the cockatiel ( is, are ) Tadd's choice for a pet.


**DIRECT OBJECTS:**

   **Delete any prepositional phrases.  Underline the subject once and the verb or verb phrase twice.  Label any direct objects – D.O.:**

4. At the grand opening of the store, the owner gave pens to his customers.


**SIMPLE/COMPOUND/COMPLEX SENTENCES:**

**A compound sentence contains two (or more) independent clauses (complete thoughts).**

   Example:   Her arms are slender, but she is very strong.
   *independent clause          independent clause*

**A complex sentence contains one independent clause and one (or more) dependent clause.**

   Example:   Although the pail is cracked, we can still use it.
   *dependent clause          independent clause*

   **Write C if the sentence is compound; write CX if the sentence is complex:**

5. A. _____    After she wrote a check, she entered the amount in the ledger.
   B. _____    She has had laryngitis for a few days, but her voice is returning.


**SENTENCE COMBINING:**

6. Troy's brother and sister ate all of the cookies.
   The cookies were chocolate chip.
   Troy had just baked them.

   _____

   _____

**DAY 128**

**CAPITALIZATION:**

1.  last summer, mother made french onion soup for our fourth of july celebration.

**PUNCTUATION:**

2.  Jack didnt win his sister did

**PARTS OF SPEECH:     VERBS**

   **Write the following:**

3.  A.   the present participle of *to drive* - _____

    B.   the past participle of *to drive* - (has, have, had) _____

**PARTS OF SPEECH:     NOUNS/ADJECTIVES**

   **Write N if the underlined word serves as a noun; write A if the underlined word serves as an adjective:**

4.  A.  _____   Courtney received a <u>rose</u> in a vase.
    B.  _____   The florist made a <u>rose</u> corsage.
    C.  _____   A customer ate a <u>potato</u> topped with sour cream.
    D.  _____   <u>Potato</u> soup with clams is tasty.

**SIMPLE/COMPOUND/COMPLEX SENTENCES:**

   **Finish these complex sentences:**

5.  A.  You may not go unless _____

    B.  Before you learn to drive, _____

**SENTENCE COMBINING:**

6.  The Zuni Indians live in New Mexico.
    They are known for their pottery.
    They are known for their jewelry.
    They are known for their weaving.

    _____

    _____

**CAPITALIZATION:**

1.  on february 23, 2000, governor ryan of illinois released funds for the pullman historic site in chicago.

**PUNCTUATION:**

2.  The newspaper article entitled Eat Out was written by Gina Liss a food editor

**PARTS OF SPEECH:    NOUNS**
   **Write the possessive form:**

3.  A.  a ball belonging to two girls - _____
    B.  balloons belonging to his sister - _____
    C.  a cage belonging to more than one mouse - _____

**PARTS OF SPEECH:    VERBS**
   **Delete any prepositional phrases.  Underline the subject once and the verb or verb phrase twice:**

4.  Has Talley shared her ice cream with her little brother?

**SPELLING:**
   **Two-syllable words ending with consonant + vowel + consonant (CVC) usually just add any suffix.  However, if the last syllable is accented, the final consonant is often doubled.**        Example:  re fer´+ ing = referring

   **Write the correct spelling of these words:**

5.  A.  begin + er - _____

    B.  deter + ed - _____

    C.  forgot + en - _____

**SENTENCE COMBINING:**

6.  The Cleveland bay is an English horse.
    It has a reddish brown body.
    It has a black mane.

    _____

    _____

**DAY 130**

**CAPITALIZATION:**

1.  "on inauguration day in 1789, george washington, placing his hands on a *bible*, took an oath," said loni.

**PUNCTUATION:**

2.  In the story entitled The Gift of the Magi Dellas hair is cut and sold

**PARTS OF SPEECH:**

3.  What part of speech is *Oh!?* _____

**PARTS OF SPEECH: VERBS**

  **Write the verb tense:**

4.  A.  future of *to be* - _____

    B.  past of *to deliver* - _____

    C.  past of *to lie* (meaning to rest ) - _____

    D.  past perfect of *to bring* - _____

**ANALOGIES:**

  **Circle the answer that best completes the analogy:**

5.  stagnant : fresh :: subtle : _____
    (a) obvious      (b) certain      (c) partial      (d) wise

**SENTENCE COMBINING:**

6.  Ken measured the beam.
    Ken cut it into two pieces.
    Each piece was identical

    _____

    _____

**CAPITALIZATION:**

1. "my parents," said pedro, "saw several whales off na pali coast in hawaii."

**PUNCTUATION:**

2. Your belief without a doubt was expressed in a clear and concise manner

**PARTS OF SPEECH:    ADVERBS**

   **Circle the correct form:**

3. A. Of all the four-wheel drives, this one runs ( more smoothly, most smoothly ).

   B. That pole vaulter jumps ( more confidently, most confidently ) than his competitor.

   C. Of all the machines in the office, this copier runs ( more efficiently, most efficiently ).

**LIBRARY:**

4. A. A/An _____ is a book of maps.

   B. Books that are true are called _____.

**SPELLING:**

   **Write the correct spelling of these words:**

5. A. scan + ing - _____

   B. prefer + ed - _____

   C. bray + ing - _____

**SENTENCE COMBINING:**

6. William of Normandy invaded England.
   He arrived with a fleet of ships.
   The year was 1066.

   _____

   _____

**DAY 132**

**CAPITALIZATION:**

1.  is sanskrit, one of the oldest languages, from india?


**PUNCTUATION:**
   **Punctuate this inside address and salutation of a business letter:**

2.  Bradley Corporation Inc
    222 Dow St
    Las Vegas NV   87701

    Dear Gentlemen


**CLAUSES:**
**Remember**:  An independent clause contains a subject and verb; it can stand alone as a sentence.
              A dependent clause contains a subject and verb, but it cannot stand alone as a sentence.

   **Write IC if the clause is independent; write DC if the clause is dependent.**

3.  A.  _____      Because I'm sick.

    B.  _____      They can't decide where to go today.


**PARTS OF SPEECH:    CONJUNCTIONS**
   **Write a sentence containing two conjunctions:**

4.  _____

    _____


**ANALOGIES:**
   **Circle the answer that best completes the analogy:**

5.  increase : dwindle :: originate : _____
    (a) terminate     (b) introduce     (c) restrain     (d) probe


**SENTENCE COMBINING:**

6.  Steven likes to play ice hockey.
    Steven likes to play field hockey.
    Steven does not like to play football.

    _____

    _____

**CAPITALIZATION:**

1.  she has a painting, <u>going home</u>, by mark silversmith, a navajo artist.

**PUNCTUATION:**
  **Punctuate these titles:**

2.  A.  (magazine article)  The High Road to the Highlands

   B.  (chapter)  The Pacific States Today

   C.  (magazine)  Fancy Cars

   D.  (play)  Oklahoma

**SENTENCES/RUN-ONS:**
  **Write <u>S</u> for a sentence; write <u>R-O</u> for a run-on sentence:**

3.  A.  _____  After the game, some friends met at Huck's house for a picnic.

   B.  _____  He showered, shaved, and ate breakfast, then he went to work and
          worked until 8 o'clock.

   C.  _____  They were very thirsty; they drank from their canteens.

**DIFFICULT WORDS:**
  **Select the correct word:**

4.  A.  Tate has ( brung, brought ) his cat along.
   B.  ( Can, May ) I help you with that?
   C.  ( You're, Your ) the best swimmer I know.

**ANALOGIES:**
  **Circle the answer that best completes the analogy:**

5.  basic : fundamental :: fashionable : _____
   (a) model      (b) eloquent      (c) chic      (d) eligible

**SENTENCE COMBINING:**

6.  Penguins walk awkwardly on dry land.
   Penguins swim smoothly.

   _____

   _____

**DAY 134**

**CAPITALIZATION:**

1.   the building of the grand canal in the orient began under emperor yang di.

**PUNCTUATION:**

2.   Shari exclaimed  Wow Weve done it again Mother

**PARTS OF SPEECH:    ADVERBS**

   **Write the seven adverbs that tell to what extent:**

3.   A.  s_____          C.  v_____          E.  r_____          G.  s_____
     B.  n_____            D.  t_____            F.  q_____

**PARTS OF SPEECH:    PRONOUNS**

   **Circle the correct pronoun:**

4.   "( We, Us ) adults must pay full fare,"  said Mrs. Slidell.

**SENTENCES:**

   **Write <u>DC</u> if the clause is dependent; write <u>IC</u> if the clause is independent:**

5.   A.   _____     If you agree to help us.
     B.   _____     Tate agreed to help us.

**SENTENCE COMBINING:**

6.   Rob Roy was an outlaw.
     He lived in Scotland.
     His real name was Robert MacGregor.

     _____

     _____

**CAPITALIZATION:**

1.  did aunt ali travel by the urubamba river to visit the ancient ruins of machu picchu?

**PUNCTUATION:**
    **Punctuate these titles:**

2.  A.  (album)  Serenades          C.  (poem)  Conestoga Wagons

    B.  (song)  London Bridges       D.  (book)  The Red Badge of Courage

**PARTS OF SPEECH:    NOUNS**
    **Write C if the noun is concrete; write A if the noun is abstract:**

3.  A.  ____  hair          C.  ____  promise          E.  ____  tub
    B.  ____  kindness       D.  ____  faith            F.  ____  smoke

**PARTS OF SPEECH:    VERBS**
    **Write the present, past, and past participle of each infinitive:**

4.  A.  to demand - _____
    B.  to swim - _____
    C.  to fly - _____

**SIMPLE/COMPOUND/COMPLEX SENTENCES:**
**A compound sentence contains two (or more) independent clauses (complete thoughts).**

> Example:    Kami studied the menu, but she couldn't make up her mind.
> _independent clause        independent clause_

**A complex sentence contains one independent clause and one (or more) dependent clause.**

> Example:    We will need to buy gas before we drive to the airport.
> _independent clause              dependent clause_

    **Write C if the sentence is compound; write CX if the sentence is complex:**

5.  A.  ____    After she wrote a check, she entered the amount in her ledger.
    B.  ____    She has had laryngitis for a few days, but her voice is returning.

**SENTENCE COMBINING:**

6.  Tuna may also be called tunney.
    It is the largest fish of the mackerel family.

    _____

    _____

**DAY 136**

**CAPITALIZATION:**

1. hank and i went on a ship, <u>southern spirit</u>, to see the otago peninsula in new zealand.

**PUNCTUATION:**

2. Mr Lopezs cousin   said Jan   lives in that three story house

**PARTS OF SPEECH:    VERBS**
   **Delete any prepositional phrases.  Underline the subject once and the verb
   or verb phrase twice:**

3. Go into the bathroom and brush your teeth.

**PARTS OF SPEECH:    NOUNS**

   **Write the plural of the following nouns:**

4.  A.  song = _____     D.  calf = _____

    B.  cactus = _____    E.  sister-in-law = _____

    C.  bayberry = _____  F.  proof = _____

**SIMPLE/COMPOUND/COMPLEX SENTENCES:**
   **Finish these complex sentences:**

5.  A.  If you have finished eating, _____

    B.  Lou is my cousin who _____

**SENTENCE COMBINING:**

6.  Lacy took her little brother's hand.
    She pulled him toward her.
    She smiled at the same time.

    _____

    _____

**CAPITALIZATION:**

1.  the alpine garden society featured colesboune park for its snowdrops, a type of flower.

**PUNCTUATION:**

2.
                                               3497 S Rosedale Dr
                                               Shelbyville TN   37160
                                               Oct 10  20--

   Dear Monica
            Weve been planning a trip to Toronto Canada for next summer
                                               Your college roommate
                                               Nanette

**PARTS OF SPEECH:   VERBS**
   **List eight linking verbs:**

3.  A. to _____      C. to _____      E. to _____      G. to _____

   B. to _____      D. to _____      F. to _____      H. to _____

**PARTS OF SPEECH:   ADVERBS**
   **Write the following sentence correctly:**

4.  He doesn't hardly have time to do nothing. _____

   _____

**SPELLING:**
   **Write the correct spelling of these words:**

5.  A.  margin + al - _____

   B.  polite + ness - _____

**SENTENCE COMBINING:**

6.  Ricardo's cousin lives on a ranch.
   It is a cattle ranch.
   He lives in Montana.
   His cousin is coming to visit Ricardo next week.

   _____

   _____

**DAY 138**

**CAPITALIZATION:**
   **Capitalize this outline:**

1.   i.   famous explorers

        a.   magellan

        b.   columbus

             1.   life

             2.   voyages

                  a.   first discovery

                  b.   other voyages

**PUNCTUATION:**

2.   Judith Viorsts poem named If I Were in Charge of the World is a short humorous one

**SENTENCE TYPES:**
   **Write the sentence type and use correct end punctuation:**

3.   A.   _____   Have you seen the volcano near Gallup
     B.   _____   Wow!  A lizard is in the garden
     C.   _____   The moving van has pulled off the road
     D.   _____   Please rinse your cereal bowl

**ALPHABETIZING:**
   **Write these words in alphabetical order:**    lint, lain, ladder, lantern, lime, lattice

4.   (a) _____   (c) _____   (e) _____
     (b) _____   (d) _____   (f) _____

**ANALOGIES:**
   **Circle the answer that best completes the analogy:**

5.   stormy : turbulent :: bizarre : _____
     (a) food      (b) selling      (c) normal      (d) weird

**SENTENCE COMBINING:**

6.   Isaac Asimov was a biochemist.
     Isaac Asimov was best known as a science fiction writer.

     _____

     _____

**CAPITALIZATION:**
   **Capitalize this letter:**

1.

                                                        1257 west hearn road
          **(A)**             edmund, oklahoma   73013
                                            march 10, 20--

**(B)**    dear camille,
             last week my family and i stayed at hamilton inn on the way to luby bay
**(C)**    near nordham, idaho.
                        **(D)**             truly yours,
                        **(E)**             jeff

**PUNCTUATION:**

2.   Because the baby is ill he is upset cranky and crying

**FRIENDLY LETTER:**
   **Label the friendly letter parts in number 1:**

3.  A. _____       D. _____
     B. _____       E. _____
     C. _____

**SUBJECT/VERB:**
   **Delete any prepositional phrases.  Underline the subject once and the verb or verb phrase twice:**

4.   One of the flags is on the wrong side of the podium.

**SPELLING:**
   **Write the correct spelling of these words:**

5.  A.  span + ing - _____

     B.  forgot + en - _____

     C.  warranty + s - _____

**SENTENCE COMBINING:**

6.   Linen was brought to northern Europe by Romans.
     Linen was the chief cloth of the Middle Ages.

    _____

    _____

**DAY 140**

**CAPITALIZATION:**

1. on presidents' day, jake went to picacho pass, site of a confederate skirmish.

**PUNCTUATION:**

2. Two thirds of the three contestants winnings will go to charity

**PARTS OF SPEECH:    PREPOSITIONS**
   List forty prepositions:

3. _____

   _____

   _____

**PREFIXES/ROOTS/SUFFIXES:**
   **Write the prefix, the root, and the suffix of *preoccupied:***

4.   A.  prefix = _____      B.  root = _____      C.  suffix = _____

**ANALOGIES:**

   **Circle the answer that best completes the analogy:**

5.   organ : heart :: flag : _____
     (a) banner    (b) wave    (c) pole    (d) flying

**SENTENCE COMBINING:**

6.   Bobby is limping.
     Bobby twisted his knee.
     Bobby fell off his mountain bike.

     _____

     _____

**CAPITALIZATION:**

1.   loren asked, "did president carter sign all bills in the oval office?"

**PUNCTUATION:**

2.   If youre ready for a game lets play Scrabble Monopoly or Rummicub

**PARTS OF SPEECH:    PRONOUNS**
   **Circle the pronoun that agrees with the antecedent:**

3.   Those children gave ( her, their ) uncle a hat.

**ANTONYMS/SYNONYMS/HOMONYMS:**

4.   A.   An antonym for *excited* is _____.
     B.   A synonym for *tidy* is _____.
     C.   A homonym for *sight* is _____.

**SIMPLE/COMPOUND/COMPLEX SENTENCES:**
   **Write a simple sentence:**

5.   _____

**SENTENCE COMBINING:**

6.   Ginger is grown for its root.
     The root is often dried for medicine.
     The root is often dried for spice.

     _____

     _____

**DAY 142**

**CAPITALIZATION:**

1. "the united states senate," remarked lani, "has two senators from each state."

**PUNCTUATION:**

2. Chet E Frampton Ph D teaches part time at a small private university

**PARTS OF SPEECH:    PRONOUNS**

**Nominative pronouns serve as either subject or predicate nominative.**
Examples:    **She** enjoys lasagna.    (subject)
The speaker was **she**.    (predicate nominative)

3. Nominative pronouns include _____, _____, _____, _____, _____,

_____, _____, and _____.

**PARTS OF SPEECH:    NOUNS**
**Write the possessive form:**

4.   A.   a friend belonging to Carrie - _____

B.   the cap on a pencil - _____

C.   pencils shared by two secretaries - _____

D.   a rabbit belonging to two toddlers - _____

**ANALOGIES:**

**Circle the answer that best completes the analogy:**

5.   happiness : gloom :: order : _____
(a) command      (b) chaos      (c) arrangement      (d) request

**SENTENCE COMBINING:**

6.   Crusaders traveled to the Middle East during the Middle Ages.
They brought back perfume to Europe.
They brought back soaps to Europe.

_____

_____

**CAPITALIZATION:**

1. her family attends beth david synagogue in northern new york," said alex.

**PUNCTUATION:**

2. Billie C Combe  D V S vaccinates our animals and examines them thoroughly

**PARTS OF SPEECH:    ADVERBS/ADJECTIVES**

 **Circle the correct word:**

3. A.  Write your name ( legible, legibly ).

    B.  A carpenter hammered the nail ( hard, hardly ).

    C.  He speaks ( loud, loudly ).

**PARTS OF SPEECH:    PRONOUNS**

 **Objective pronouns serve as direct objects, indirect objects, or objects of prepositions.**    Examples:   The waiter bumped **me** with a tray.   (direct object)
They tossed **me** a ball.   (indirect object)
Come with **me**.   (object of the preposition)

4.  Objective pronouns are _____, _____, _____, _____, _____, _____, _____, and _____.

**SPELLING:**

 **Write the correct spelling of the following words:**

5. A.  biography + s - _____

    B.  jolly + ness - _____

    C.  shame + ful - _____

**SENTENCE COMBINING:**

6.  The cashew nut grows at the end of a stalk.
    This stalk is shaped like a pear.
    This stalk is called a cashew apple.

    _____

    _____

**DAY 144**

**CAPITALIZATION:**

**Capitalize these titles:**

1.   A.   <u>highlights for children</u>

      B.   "race against death"

      C.   "improve your health care"

**PUNCTUATION:**

2.   The movie entitled Camelot tells of King Arthurs reign  said Casey

**PREFIXES/ROOTS/SUFFIXES:**

*Anti,* **a prefix, means against.**

3.   Write a word using *anti* and tell the meaning of the word: _____

_____

**PARTS OF SPEECH:     VERBS**

**Write the verb tense:**

4.   A.   _____   I **met** our senator last week.

      B.   _____   I **meet** my friend each Monday.

      C.   _____   I **shall meet** with you next week.

**ANALOGIES:**

**Circle the answer that best completes the analogy:**

5.   wet : arid :: erratic : _____
     (a) livid     (b) consistent     (c) erasable     (d) happy

**SENTENCE COMBINING:**

6.   A man who is knighted is called Sir.
     A knighted woman is called Dame.

_____

_____

**CAPITALIZATION:**

1.  john ciardi, a poet, graduated from tufts university and served in the united states army air corp.

**PUNCTUATION:**

2.  Yes he most certainly will be the lead actor the star of the play

**PARTS OF SPEECH:    ADVERB/PREPOSITION**
   **Write A if the boldfaced word serves as an adverb; write P if the boldfaced word serves as a preposition:**

3.  A.  _____    Playing a game, the children ran **around** in a circle.
    B.  _____    The police ran **around** the side of the abandoned building.

**PARTS OF SPEECH:    ADJECTIVES**
   **Circle any descriptive adjectives:**

4.  At the family picnic, they ate fried chicken, potato salad, and chocolate cake.

**SIMPLE/COMPOUND/COMPLEX SENTENCES:**

**A compound sentence contains two (or more) independent clauses (complete thoughts).**
   Example:   Her arms are slender, but she is very strong.
                        *independent clause        independent clause*

**A complex sentence contains one independent clause and one (or more) dependent clause.**
   Example:   Although the pail is cracked, we can still use it.
                       *dependent clause        independent clause*

**Write C if the sentence is compound; write CX if the sentence is complex:**

5.  A.  ____    If you agree, we'll meet tomorrow.
    B.  ____    She chopped onions, and her friend grated cheese.

**SENTENCE COMBINING:**

6.  Great Bear Lake is the largest lake in Canada.
    It is ice-bound for eight months of the year.

    _____

    _____

# DAY 146

## CAPITALIZATION:
**Capitalize this letter:**

1.

          **(A)**       77 east sunnyside drive
                         scottsdale az   85254
                         april 1 20--

**(B)**    dear mrs redford
          this letter is to let you know that i really enjoyed your math class when i
**(C)**    was in fifth grade  mr bencze is having us write a note to a former teacher and i
        have chosen you  thanks for your help
                     **(D)**        sincerely yours
                     **(E)**        bruno rociola

## PUNCTUATION:

2.   Punctuate the friendly letter in #1.

## FRIENDLY LETTER:
**Label the friendly letter parts:**

3.  A. _____       D. _____
     B. _____       E. _____
     C. _____

## PARTS OF SPEECH:    PRONOUNS
**Circle the correct pronoun:**

4.   Janie and Justin gave ( they, them ) several tickets to a Cinco de Mayo celebration.

## SPELLING:
**Words ending in the sound *er* usually have a spelling of <u>or</u> if *ion* or *tion* can be added to the base word:**     Example:   crea<u>tion</u> - crea<u>tor</u>

**Write the word, adding the correct *er* spelling of the following words:**

5.  A. distribute - _____
     B. organize  - _____
     C. protect - _____

## SENTENCE COMBINING:

6.   Marcy is an architect.
     She is designing an office building.

_____

_____

**CAPITALIZATION:**

**Capitalize this portion of a poem entitled "Silver" by Walter De La Mare:**

1.  slowly, silently, now the moon

    walks the night in her silver shoon;

    this way, and that, she peers, and sees

    silver fruit upon silver trees.

**PUNCTUATION:**

2.  Evans friend the boy in the blue swimsuit has won twenty one medals for swim

    ming and diving events

**ANTONYMS/SYNONYMS/HOMONYMS:**

3.  A.  A synonym for *angry* is _____.
    B.  An antonym for *shy* is _____.
    C.  A homonym for *pain* is _____.

**PARTS OF SPEECH:   PREPOSITIONS**

   **Circle any object of the preposition:**

4.  The nylon jacket with a hood has a patch on the left sleeve.

**ANALOGIES:**

   **Circle the answer that best completes the analogy:**

5.  devise : create  :: implore : _____
    (a) beg      (b) revolt      (c) discern      (d) demand

**SENTENCE COMBINING:**

6.  Deka is making a cup of cocoa.
    She is pouring milk into a mug.
    The milk is hot.
    The mug is glass.

    _____

    _____

**DAY 148**

**CAPITALIZATION:**

1.  in washington, d. c., we crossed arlington memorial bridge and continued east by the korean veterans' memorial.

**PUNCTUATION:**

2.  She now resides at 1 Watts Avenue Suite 22A Goldsboro NC  27533

**PARTS OF SPEECH:    VERBS**
  **Write the contraction:**

3.  A. where is - _____     E. do not - _____     I. I have -_____

    B. I will - _____     F. might not - _____     J. cannot - _____

    C. they are - _____     G. I would - _____     K. it is - _____

    D. must not - _____     H. we are - _____     L. you will - _____

**PARTS OF SPEECH:    PRONOUNS**

4.  The possessive pronouns are _____, _____, _____, _____, _____,

    _____, _____, _____, _____, _____, _____, _____, and _____.

**SPELLING:**

  **Write the correct spelling of the following words:**

5.  A.  refuse + al - _____

    B.  negative + ity - _____

    C.  strut + ed - _____

**SENTENCE COMBINING:**

6.  William Ramsey was a British chemist.
    He discovered argon.
    He discovered neon.
    He discovered krypton.

    _____

    _____

**CAPITALIZATION:**

1. is the painting, <u>a garden behind the fence</u>, at toho gallery in philadelphia?

**PUNCTUATION:**

2. Patsys name has been misspelled on the trophy however shell keep it

**WORDS:**
  **Circle the correct word:**

3. A. They studied the ( affect, effect ) color has on moods.
   B. They are planning on going ( irregardless, regardless ) of the weather.
   C. ( Their, There, They're ) reaction was hilarious.
   D. This table would look great in ( you're, your ) kitchen.

**FRIENDLY LETTERS/ENVELOPES:**
  **Write your return address on this envelope:**

4. _____

   _____

   _____

   _____

                          Ms. Mona Martinez
                          11111 Pine Street
                          Warrensburg, MO   64093

_____

**SIMPLE/COMPOUND/COMPLEX SENTENCES:**
  **Finish this compound sentence:**

5. Her grandfather is coming today, but _____

**SENTENCE COMBINING:**

6. Ben Franklin proved that lightning is electrical.
   He proved it in a kite experiment.
   The experiment was very dangerous.

   _____

   _____

**DAY 150**

**CAPITALIZATION:**

1.  becky and i took chief joseph scenic highway through sunlight basin in montana.

**PUNCTUATION:**

2.  Miss Sabo asked  Is this doughnut  one half gram of fat  on your new diet

**DICTIONARY:    ALPHABETIZING**

   **Write these words in alphabetical order:**

3.  fry, farthing, fright, first, fruit, freight: _____

   _____

**PARTS OF SPEECH:    PRONOUNS**

   **Circle the correct pronoun:**

4.  The artist who drew that cartoon is ( she, her ) in the blue suit.

**ANALOGIES:**

   **Circle the answer that best completes the analogy:**

5.  sports : golf :: ship : _____
       (a) sailcloth    (b) stern    (c) yacht    (d) rigging

**SENTENCE COMBINING:**

6.  The ride was fast.
    The ride was at an amusement park.
    Lulu became dizzy.

   _____

   _____

**CAPITALIZATION:**

1. "did the homestead act," asked dr. topaz, "offer pioneers free land in nebraska?"

**PUNCTUATION:**

2. Although my brother in law cant attend the wedding hes sending a gift

**SENTENCES/FRAGMENTS/RUN-ONS:**
   Write <u>S</u> for sentence, <u>F</u> for fragment, and <u>R-O</u> for run-on:

3. A. _____ Janice at the window.

   B. _____ Janice stood silently at the window.

   C. _____ Janice stood silently at the window, her head was lowered.

   D. _____ Janice stood silently at the window and watched the children playing in the street but didn't call out to them but just smiled at them and then sighed.

**PARTS OF SPEECH:   VERBS**
   Write <u>A</u> if the verb is action; write <u>L</u> if the verb is linking:

4. A. _____ Harriet <u>grew</u> two bell pepper plants in her garden.

   B. _____ Henry <u>grew</u> tired of sitting still during the ceremony.

**SIMPLE/COMPOUND/COMPLEX SENTENCES:**

   Write <u>S</u> if the sentence is simple; write <u>C</u> if the sentence is compound:

5. A. _____ Nora made waffles, and her sister made a coffee cake.

   B. _____ After the second quarter of the game, we were ready to leave.

**SENTENCE COMBINING:**

6. Quasars are heavenly objects.
   They are faint blue.
   They are believed to be the most distant objects in the universe.

   _____

   _____

**DAY 152**

**CAPITALIZATION:**

1.  from 175 – 164 b. c., judas maccabeus, a jewish patriot, became a leader.

**PUNCTUATION:**

2.  At 3 30 in the morning the Soaring Eagle* landed at Racine Wisconsin

*name of an airplane

**DIRECT OBJECTS/INDIRECT OBJECTS/OBJECTS OF THE PREPOSITION:**
Write <u>D.O.</u> if the boldfaced word serves as a direct object, <u>I.O.</u> if the boldfaced word serves as an indirect object, and <u>O.P.</u> if the boldfaced word serves as an object of the preposition:

3.  A. _____ A waitress served **us** apple pie with cheese.
    B. _____ They cut the **tree** into logs for the fire.
    C. _____ Don't leave without your **umbrella**.

**ENVELOPE:**
Write your return address on the envelope.  Address the letter to the Barrett Company at 562 Lind Lane in Tyler, Texas   75701.

4. _____

   _____

   _____

   _____

                                        _____

                                        _____

                                        _____

   _____

**ANALOGIES:**
Circle the answer that best completes the analogy:

5.  device : can opener :: pasta : _____
    (a) macaroni      (b) Italian      (c) food      (d) delicious

**SENTENCE COMBINING:**

6.  Cape Horn is located at the tip of South America.
    It is known for its strong currents.
    It is also known for its stormy weather.

    _____

    _____

**CAPITALIZATION:**

1.   was barry goldwater, a former u. s. senator from arizona, a republican?

**PUNCTUATION:**

2.   No Mr Kartle we wont need the following   staples tape or paper clips

**PARTS OF SPEECH:   VERBS**
   **Select the correct verb:**

3.   A.   ( Can, May ) I help you?

   B.   ( Can, May ) you do that yourself?

   C.   The student has ( brought, brung ) his pet for a demonstrative speech.

   D.   A toddler had ( swam, swum ) across the pool by himself.

**PREFIXES/ROOTS/SUFFIXES:**

   **The roots, *ped* and *pod*, mean foot.**
   ***Terra*, a root, means earth or ground.**

   Using this information, write the meanings of the following words:

4.   A.   pedestrian - _____

   B.   terrarium - _____

   C.   podiatrist - _____

**SIMPLE/COMPOUND/COMPLEX SENTENCES:**

   **Finish this compound sentence:**

5.   Logan must take the bus, or_____

**SENTENCE COMBINING:**

6.   The whelk is a large marine animal.
   It feeds on crabs.
   It also feeds on lobster.

   _____

   _____

**DAY 154**

**CAPITALIZATION:**

1.  cattle called zebus, sometimes used for riding in india, are also raised in north america.

**PUNCTUATION:**

2.  When you write winter youll need to be sure to cross the t

**PARTS OF SPEECH:    VERBS**
   **Write the verb tense:**

3.  A.   past tense of *to wipe* - _____

    B.   future tense of *to remove* - _____

    C.   present tense of *to scrub* - _____

    D.   past tense of *to throw* - _____

**PARTS OF SPEECH:    ADJECTIVES**
   **Circle any limiting adjectives:**

4.  Many tourists rode on two buses to the wilderness area.

**SPELLING:**
   **Write the correct spelling of these words:**

5.  A.   cool + ant - _____

    B.   classify + ed - _____

    C.   notice + able - _____

**SENTENCE COMBINING:**

6.  The traffic began to slow.
    This happened suddenly.
    The traffic was on the freeway.
    Some motorists took the next exit.

    _____

    _____

**CAPITALIZATION:**

1.   when touring a japanese city, she visited asakusa kannon temple and nijo castle.

**PUNCTUATION:**

2.   Two thirds of the class watched Where the Red Fern Grows while the others finished their books

**PARTS OF SPEECH:    VERBS**
    **Write the tense of the verb (present, past, or future):**

3.   A.   _____   The mail lady delivered our letters early.
     B.   _____   Our dentist will take X-rays.
     C.   _____   They often swim in a pond.
     D.   _____   I shall give this to the owner.

**PHRASES/CLAUSES:**
    **Write P for phrase and C for clause:**

4.   A.   _____   She sneezed.          C.   _____   Brushing his teeth.
     B.   _____   After he washed his car.   D.   _____   Without a leash.

**ANALOGIES:**

  **Circle the answer that best completes the analogy:**

5.   waste : conserve :: join : _____
     (a) coincide    (b) unite    (c) merge    (d) sever

**SENTENCE COMBINING:**

6.   Fiberglass is made of thread.
     It is made from hot glass.
     Hot glass is forced through a sieve.

     _____

     _____

**DAY 156**

**CAPITALIZATION:**
**Capitalize these lines from Edna St. Vincent Millay's poem, "The Fawn":**

1. he lay, yet there he lay,

    asleep on the moss, his head on his polished cleft, small ebony hooves,

    the child of the doe, the dappled child of the deer.

**PUNCTUATION:**
**Punctuate these titles:**

2.  A. (newspaper article) Cowboy Sunset        C. (magazine) Motor Boating and Sailing
    B. (television show) Home Today            D. (movie) 202 Beagles

**PARTS OF SPEECH:    ADVERBS**
**Circle any adverbs:**

3.  Yesterday, we didn't ride on that rather old Ferris wheel.

**PARTS OF SPEECH:    ADJECTIVES**
**Circle any adjectives:**

4.  Those four new chairs in the living room are soft and comfortable.

**ANALOGIES:**

**Circle the answer that best completes the analogy:**

5.  cargo : freight :: attack : _____
    (a) victim        (b) crime        (c) assault        (d) response

**SENTENCE COMBINING:**

6.  Pago Pago is a seaport.
    Pago Pago is located on Tutuila Island.
    Tutuila Island is part of American Samoa.

    _____

    _____

**CAPITALIZATION:**

1.  at the louvre, a museum in paris, france, i saw venus de milo which was sculpted in

    140 b. c.


**PUNCTUATION:**
   **Write the abbreviation:**

2.  A.  column - _____     D.  street - _____

    B.  centimeter - _____    E.  corporation - _____

    C.  quart - _____       F.  mile - _____


**PARTS OF SPEECH:    ADJECTIVES/ADVERBS**
   **Write the adjective and the adverb form for each noun:**
   *ADJECTIVE*                                    *ADVERB*

3.  A.  ice - _____    _____
    B.  danger - _____   _____
    C.  kindness - _____    _____
    D.  intelligence - _____    _____


**LIBRARY SKILLS:**

4.  A.  A book of maps is called a/an _____.
    B.  Current information and statistics can be found in a/an _____.
    C.  A _____ dictionary gives information about famous people.
    D.  A _____ dictionary gives information about important places.


**ANALOGIES:**

   **Circle the answer that best completes the analogy:**

5.  Japan : teriyaki  :: China : _____
    (a) sushi     (b) chow mien     (c) cooking     (d) sukiyaki


**SENTENCE COMBINING:**

6.  Tom is writing an essay.
    It is about the French and Indian War.
    Tom is nearly finished.

    _____

    _____

**DAY 158**

**CAPITALIZATION:**

1. are you on the mailing list of lido christian college in austria?


**PUNCTUATION:**

2. Although Miller Schools committee met on Tuesday no financial decision was made


**PARTS OF SPEECH:    PRONOUNS**

Circle the possessive pronoun and box its antecedent:

3. Chelsea stubbed her toe on the step.


**PARTS OF SPEECH:    VERBS**

Write the correct form:

| | | Present | Past | Past Participle |
|---|---|---|---|---|
| 4. | A. to do | _____ | _____ | _____ |
| | B. to believe | _____ | _____ | _____ |
| | C. to burst | _____ | _____ | _____ |


**SIMPLE/COMPOUND/COMPLEX SENTENCES:**

Write **C** if the sentence is compound; write **CX** if the sentence is complex:

5. A. _____ Leave early, or you may encounter heavy traffic.
   B. _____ When the alarm clock rang, I turned it off.


**SENTENCE COMBINING:**

6. Janie went to the zoo.
   Janie went with her family.
   They then went to a fast-food restaurant for lunch.

   _____

   _____

**CAPITALIZATION:**

1.  was the treaty called peace of ulbrecht the one in which the english said that the iroquois indians were british subjects?

**PUNCTUATION:**

2.  Your dog a beagle is lovable frisky and funny

**PARTS OF SPEECH:    ADVERBS**
 **Write this sentence in two correct ways:**

 *He is not scheduled for nothing.*

3.  A.  _____

 B.  _____

**DICTIONARY:    GUIDE WORDS**
 **Write <u>Yes</u> if the words can be found with the following guide words; write <u>No</u> if the words cannot be found on a dictionary page with those guide words:**

 **eggplant          elephant**

4.  A.  ____ egg     B.  ____ eighty     C.  ____ elegant     D.  ____ emphasize

**SENTENCES/FRAGMENTS/RUN-ONS:**
 **Write <u>S</u> for sentence, <u>F</u> for fragment, and <u>R-O</u> on run-on:**

5.  A.  ____     Their parents are leaving they are going to the airport.

 B.  ____     Ms. Jacobs gone to Viet Nam.

**SENTENCE COMBINING:**

6.  Lovage is a plant.
 It is native to southern Europe.
 It is used in cooking.

 _____

 _____

**DAY 160**

**CAPITALIZATION:**

1.  the authority of parliament in england was established by the settlement act of 1701.

**PUNCTUATION:**

2.  Wow  Youre the first place runner  exclaimed the coachs assistant

**PARTS OF SPEECH:    VERBS**

   **Select the correct verb:**

3.  Either this watch or those clocks ( operates, operate ) on batteries.

**PARTS OF SPEECH:    NOUNS**

   **Write two sentences.  In the first sentence, use _CUBS_ as a common noun.  In the second sentence, use _CUBS_ as a proper noun:**

4.  A.  _____

   _____

   B.  _____

   _____

**SPELLING:**
   **Write the correct spelling of the following words:**

5.  A.  pressure + ize - _____

   B.  cruel + ty - _____

   C.  measure + able - _____

**SENTENCE COMBINING:**

6.  The Shetland Islands are located off northern Scotland.
   The Shetland pony comes from there.
   The Shetland sheepdog comes from there.

   _____

   _____

**CAPITALIZATION:**

1. "thomas moran," said mrs. ving, "painted western landscapes."

**PUNCTUATION:**

2. Dr Killians neighbor said Samantha is an ex teacher from Lincoln Nebraska

**SENTENCE TYPES:**
**Write the sentence type:**

3.  A. _____ Do you need this?

    B. _____ My friend loves to read.

    C. _____ You're right!

    D. _____ Take this with you.

**PARTS OF SPEECH:    CONJUNCTIONS**
**Correlative conjunctions occur in pairs.**
    Examples:    neither – nor        either – or        both – and

**Circle any correlative conjunctions; then, place two lines under the verb that agrees:**

4.  A.  Either Tom or his sister ( has, have ) to empty the dishwasher.
    B.  Both Tom and his sister ( has, have ) to empty the dishwasher.

**SPELLING:**
**Write the correct spelling of these words:**

5.  A.  hustle + ing - _____

    B.  cram + ed - _____

    C.  enhance + ment - _____

**SENTENCE COMBINING:**

6.  Babe Ruth is considered the most famous baseball player in history.
    Babe Ruth led the Yankees to win pennants.
    The Yankees won seven pennants.

_____

_____

**DAY 162**

**CAPITALIZATION:**

1.  jay asked, "has grandma ever been to capon springs in hardy county, west virginia?"

**PUNCTUATION:**
   **Punctuate this letter:**

2.                                                          12 Oak Circle
                                    ( A )                   Alabaster AL   35007
                                                            Aug 18  20—
      ( B )      Dear Roxanne
      ( C )         Thanks for your letter  My grandparents house is just two
                 blocks from yours  When I arrive Ill call you
                       ( D )                 Sincerely
                             ( E )  Inga

**FRIENDLY LETTER:**
   **Label the parts of the friendly letter above:**

3.   A.  _____       D.  _____
     B.  _____       E.  _____
     C.  _____

**DIFFICULT WORDS:**
   **Circle the correct word:**

4.   A.   ( May, Can ) we go to the mall?
     B.   "I don't feel ( good, well )," said the child to the teacher.
     C.   Do you like ( them, those ) shoes, Misty?

**ANALOGIES:**
   **Circle the answer that best completes the analogy:**

5.   mutual : joint :: enlarge : _____
     (a) dilate      (b) diminish      (c) shrink      (d) harmless

**SENTENCE COMBINING:**

6.   The Magna Carta was a document.
     King John of England signed it.
     It was signed in 1215.

     _____

     _____

**CAPITALIZATION:**

**Capitalize this outline:**

1.  i   mid-atlantic states

      a.   geography

      b.   natural resources

   ii.  new england states

**PUNCTUATION:**

2.   The class of 1964 held a reunion at Regal Resort 22 McRay Blvd Tulsa Oklahoma

**PARTS OF SPEECH:   PRONOUNS**

3.   (Me, Todd, and Ashley) (Todd, Ashley, and me), (Todd, Ashley, and I) hike often.

**PARTS OF SPEECH:   PREPOSITIONS**

**Box any prepositional phrases; circle any objects of the preposition:**

4.   Within an hour of the robbery, a broadcast concerning the event stated that two men in a van had been captured.

**ANALOGIES:**

**Circle the answer that best completes the analogy:**

5.   yielding : resistant :: pungent : _____
    (a) spicy    (b) punishing    (c) bland    (d) secretive

**SENTENCE COMBINING:**

6.   A koala is an Australian animal.
    It dwells in trees.
    It feeds exclusively on eucalyptus leaves and buds.

_____

_____

**DAY 164**

**CAPITALIZATION:**

1.  the hubble space telescope was put into orbit from the space shuttle, <u>discovery</u>.


**PUNCTUATION:**

2.  After weve read How to Eat Fried Worms* well write a summary

*name of a book

**SUBJECT/VERB:**

**Cross out any prepositional phrases.  Underline the subject once and the verb or verb phrase twice**:

3.  A picnic site and rest area had been closed during the road construction.


**PARTS OF SPEECH:    NOUNS**

**Write the possessive:**

4.  A.   a puppy belonging to two children - _____

    B.   a rattle belonging to a baby - _____

    C.   hot dogs and buns belonging to a cook - _____

    D.   several books belonging to two teachers - _____


**SPELLING:**

**Write the correct spelling of these words:**

5.  A.   erase + ure - _____

    B.   pretty + er - _____

    C.   rasp + y - _____


**SENTENCE COMBINING:**

6.  Lucas interviewed for a job.
    The job was selling automobiles.
    Lucas was not hired.

    _____

    _____

**CAPITALIZATION:**

1.  during world war I, congress passed the eighteenth amendment to the constitution.

**PUNCTUATION:**

2.  Mrs Harrison asked  Brett does your middle name begin with a P

**PARTS OF SPEECH:     NOUNS**
   **Write the plural:**

3.   A.  woman - _____          E.  agency - _____

     B.  business - _____          F.  bandage - _____

     C.  relay - _____              G.  tax - _____

     D.  value - _____              H.  moose -_____

**PARTS OF SPEECH:     PREPOSITIONS/ADVERBS**
   **Write P if the boldfaced word is a preposition; write A if the boldfaced word is an adverb:**

4.   A.  _____    The children went **outside** to play.

     B.  _____    Please put the broom **outside** the door.

     C.  _____    The child fell **down** and skinned his knee.

     D.  _____    Two sailors walked **down** the street.

**ANALOGIES:**
   **Circle the answer that best completes the analogy:**

5.   unbelievable : credible :: immune : _____
     (a) resistant        (b) responsive        (c) immense        (d) susceptible

**SENTENCE COMBINING:**

6.   The yak is an animal of Tibet.
     It is a source of milk.
     It is a source of meat.

     _____

     _____

**DAY 166**

## CAPITALIZATION:
**Capitalize these titles:**

1. A. idaho women in business

    B. "life on a boat"

    C. the united states and its neighbors


## PUNCTUATION:

2. His son in law the man in the jacket is twenty seven years old


## PARTS OF SPEECH:   VERBS
**Write the twenty-three auxiliary (helping) verbs:**

3.     _____

       _____


## SENTENCES/FRAGMENTS/RUN-ONS:
**Write <u>S</u> for sentence, <u>F</u> for fragment, and <u>R-O</u> for run-on:**

4. A. _____ In 1947, Secretary of State Marshall that U. S. reconstruction of Europe.

    B. _____ Wait here.


## ANALOGIES:
**Circle the answer that best completes the analogy:**

5. contrived : spontaneous :: defiant : _____
   (a) determined    (b) irritable    (c) compliant    (d) preoccupied


## SENTENCE COMBINING:

6. Theo is preparing a salad.
Theo is slicing cucumbers.
Theo is slicing carrots.
Theo is slicing tomatoes.

    _____

    _____

**CAPITALIZATION:**

1. a slave to a boston merchant, phyllis wheatly became the first african-american writer in america.

**PUNCTUATION:**

2. They havent seen Mark but theyll help you look for him

**PARTS OF SPEECH:    VERBS**

   Write <u>RV</u> if the verb is regular; write <u>IV</u> if the verb is irregular:

3. A. ____ to beat       C. ____ to shake      E. ____ to fly

   B. ____ to work       D. ____ to be         F. ____ to watch

**PARTS OF SPEECH:    ADJECTIVES**

   Write the correct form:

4. A. Kristina's ring is _____ ( comparative of old ) than mine.

   B. Your idea sounds _____ ( superlative of reasonable ).

**SPELLING:**

   Write the correct spelling of these words:

5. A. crabby + ness - _____

   B. slur + ed - _____

   C. refine + ment - _____

**SENTENCE COMBINING:**

6. John Jacob Astor arrived in America penniless.
   He died in 1848.
   He was then the richest man in America.

   _____

   _____

**DAY 168**

**CAPITALIZATION:**

1.  governor maria reno, a democrat, ordered a baby gift basket for her korean friend.

**PUNCTUATION:**

2.  When the class of 91 held a picnic many couldnt attend

**PARTS OF SPEECH:    NOUNS**
   **Circle the appositive:**

3.  Their favorite hobby, collecting magnets, is unusual.

**PARTS OF SPEECH:    VERBS**
   **Write the tense:**

|         |          | *Present* | *Past* | *Past Perfect* |
|---------|----------|-----------|--------|----------------|
| 4.  A.  | to begin | _____ | _____ | _____ |
|     B.  | to run   | _____ | _____ | _____ |
|     C.  | to climb | _____ | _____ | _____ |

**SPELLING:**
   **Write the correct spelling of these words:**

5.  A.  heavy + ness - _____

    B.  sparse + ly - _____

    C.  immune + ity - _____

**SENTENCE COMBINING:**

6.  John Chapman sowed apple seeds in Ohio.
    He sowed apple seeds in Indiana.
    He sowed apple seeds in western Pennsylvania.
    He was called Johnny Appleseed.

    _____

    _____

**CAPITALIZATION:**

1.   the freer gallery, a member of the smithsonian, houses many works from the far east.

**PUNCTUATION:**

2.   The two boys father had arrived at the Queen Mary* at 130 P M

*name of a ship

**PARTS OF SPEECH:    VERBS**

3.   Write an example of an infinitive: _____

**PARTS OF SPEECH:    ADJECTIVES/NOUNS**

   **Write a sentence using *birthday* as an adjective:**

4.   A.   _____

   _____

   **Write a sentence using *birthday* as a noun:**

   B.   _____

   _____

**ANALOGIES:**

   **Circle the answer that best completes the analogy:**

5.   exact : imprecise :: significant : _____
   (a) trivial      (b) ornate      (c) relevant      (d) willful

**SENTENCE COMBINING:**

6.   Ducks can be divided into three groups.
   One group is diving.
   One group is fish-catching.
   One group is surface feeding.

   _____

   _____

**DAY 170**

**CAPITALIZATION:**

1.  in the battle of shiloh of the civil war, union troops were led by general grant.

**PUNCTUATION:**

2.  A short snappish dog  said Justin  stared at my half eaten sandwich

**PARTS OF SPEECH:**
Write <u>A</u> if the verb is action; write <u>L</u> if the verb is linking:

3.  A.  _____  The cat <u>looked</u> contented.
    B.  _____  Jana <u>looked</u> for shells at the beach.
    C.  _____  This bread pudding <u>tastes</u> delicious.
    D.  _____  That cook <u>tastes</u> all her stews.

**PREFIXES/ROOTS/SUFFIXES:**
Prefixes have meaning:

    Examples:   uni – one        tri – three       pent – five
                bi – two         quad – four       oct – eight

Using this information, write the meaning of each word; use a dictionary if necessary:

4.  A.  unicycle - _____
    B.  quadruplets - _____
    C.  pentagon - _____
    D.  octopus - _____

**SPELLING:**
Write the correct spelling of these words:

5.  A.  invoice + ing - _____

    B.  sense + ible - _____

    C.  attorney + s - _____

**SENTENCE COMBINING:**

6.  Cyrus McCormick invented the reaper.
    He also started installment buying in America.

    _____

    _____

**CAPITALIZATION:**

1.  "the nation of morocco," said allison, "is bordered on the south by the moroccan sahara.

**PUNCTUATION:**

2.  No Mr Jensen we havent seen the Spruce Goose* in Long Beach California

*name of an airplane

**PARTS OF SPEECH:    VERBS**
   **Delete any prepositional phrases.  Underline the subject once and the verb or verb phrase twice:**

3.  Go into the bathroom and brush your teeth.

**PHRASES/CLAUSES:**

   **Write IC if the clause is independent; write DC if the clause is dependent:**

4.  A. _____    The shadows cast on the mountains gave them an eerie appearance.

    B. _____    When Lincoln gave the Gettysburg Address.

    C. _____    Go at the sound of the bell.

    D. _____    If the drain will not open.

**ANALOGIES:**

   **Circle the answer that best completes the analogy:**

5.  deadlock : impasse :: magistrate : _____
    (a) marshall    (b) marriage    (c) judge    (d) magician

**SENTENCE COMBINING:**

6.  Mrs. Yassi listens to her voice mail messages.
    Mrs. Yassi takes careful notes.
    Mrs. Yassi is a nurse.
    She works in a doctor's office.

    _____

    _____

**DAY 172**

**CAPITALIZATION:**

1.   has the pan american health organization explained the health problems of the british virgin islands?

**PUNCTUATION:**

2.   When you finish knitting Shawns sweater  Ill send it for you Beth

**SENTENCES/FRAGMENTS/RUN-ONS:**
   **Write S for sentence, F for fragment, and R-O for run-on:**

3.   A.  _____   Stop.

   B.  _____   You must stop your car.

   C.  _____   Stopping his car.

   D.  _____   Stop now, I want to talk to you.

**PARTS OF SPEECH:    ADJECTIVES/ADVERBS**

   **Write *good* or *well* in the space provided:**

4.   A.  Gary plays football _____.

   B.  You are a _____ artist.

   C.  Having eaten too much, they don't feel _____.

**ANALOGIES:**

   **Circle the answer that best completes the analogy:**

5.   disagreement : feud :: acquaintance : _____
   (a) neighbor      (b) colleague      (c) friend      (d) novelty

**SENTENCE COMBINING:**

6.   Jackson Hole is in Wyoming.
   It was named after David Jackson.
   David Jackson wintered there in 1828.

   _____

   _____

**CAPITALIZATION:**

1.   was president james monroe's daughter, hester, the first to marry in the white house?

**PUNCTUATION:**

2.   Jina read her essay entitled Lucy Darraghs Courage at a D A R* meeting

*Daughters of the American Revolution organization

**PARTS OF SPEECH:    PRONOUNS**

   **Circle the correct pronoun:**

3.   A.   "This is ( she, her )," answered the voice on the telephone.

   B.   This matter is between Sandy and ( I, me ).

   C.   You must explain that to ( us, we ) students again.

**PARTS OF SPEECH:    NOUNS**
   **Write an example:**

4.   A.   concrete noun - _____

   B.   abstract noun - _____

**SPELLING:**
   **Write the correct spelling of these words:**

5.   A.   arrive + al - _____

   B.   hoist + ed - _____

   C.   alloy + s - _____

**SENTENCE COMBINING:**

6.   Lynn scooped up her puppy.
   The puppy was frisky.
   She picked him up gently.
   The telephone began to ring at the same time.

   _____

   _____

**DAY 174**

**CAPITALIZATION:**

1. did henry II sign the treaty of windsor at selskar abbey in ireland?

**PUNCTUATION:**

2. Its snowing therefore we must drive slowly and carefully

**ANTONYMS/SYNONYMS/HOMONYMS:**

3. A. A homonym for *lief* is _____.

    B. A synonym for *propose* is _____.

    C. A antonym for *descend* is _____.

**PARTS OF SPEECH:    NOUNS**
   **Circle the appositive phrase:**

4. Parker, my granddaughter, laughs frequently.

**SIMPLE/COMPOUND/COMPLEX SENTENCES:**

   **Write <u>S</u> for simple, <u>C</u> for compound, and <u>CX</u> for complex:**

5. A. _____ My grandmother is seventy-eight, and she is in great shape.
    B. _____ That raccoon lives near our stream and goes there each day.
    C. _____ My favorite relative is my aunt who has four cats.

**SENTENCE COMBINING:**

6. The minuet is a French dance.
   It was introduced into Louis XIV's court.
   It was introduced in 1650.

   _____

   _____

**CAPITALIZATION:**
   **Capitalize this outline:**

1.     i.  types of automobiles

           a.  modern vehicles

                 1.  foreign cars

                 2.  domestic cars

           b.  first discovery

       ii.  other modes of transport


**PUNCTUATION:**

2.   Have you Jacy  asked his mother  done your chores


**PARTS OF SPEECH:     NOUNS**
   **Circle any nouns:**

3.   The book covers will allow for the use of crayons, markers, or pencils.


**PARTS OF SPEECH:     ADVERBS**
   **Write the following:**

4.   A.   The comparative form of *respectfully* - _____

     B.   The superlative form of *respectfully* - _____


**ANALOGIES:**
   **Circle the answer that best completes the analogy:**

5.   ambivalent : definite :: ambiguous : _____
     (a) mammoth      (b) wavering      (c) confused      (d) clear


**SENTENCE COMBINING:**

6.   The dress is made of black velvet.
     Carla's sister designed it.
     Governor Hans bought it.

     _____

     _____

**DAY 176**

**CAPITALIZATION:**

1.  the hampton court conference of 1614 authorized the king james version of the *bible*.


**PUNCTUATION:**

2.  This cake by the way doesnt contain eggs but it does have mayonnaise


**PARTS OF SPEECH:     PRONOUNS**
   **Circle the correct pronoun:**

3.  ( We, Us ) shoppers must use that escalator.


**PARTS OF SPEECH:     NOUNS**
   **Write <u>P.N.</u> if the boldfaced word serves as a predicate nominative, <u>D.O.</u> if the boldfaced word serves as a direct object, and <u>I.O.</u> if the boldfaced word serves as an indirect object:**

4.  A.  _____     Give the supermarket **clerk** your money.

    B.  _____     Charlotte's favorite dessert is apple **pie**.

    C.  _____     The dog buried a **bone** in the backyard.


**SPELLING:**

   **Write the correct spelling of these words:**

5.  A.  precise + ness - _____

    B.  stingy + ly - _____

    C.  quote + ing - _____


**SENTENCE COMBINING:**

6.  Rococo is a style of architecture.
    It is very ornate.
    It has shell, scroll, and leaf designs.

    _____

    _____

**CAPITALIZATION:**

1.  did g. f. handel, a german composer, write a work called <u>messiah</u>?

**PUNCTUATION:**

2.  A toad an amphibian that lives mostly on land has rough warty skin

**PARTS OF SPEECH:   VERBS**

  **Select the verb that agrees with the subject:**

3.  A.   Both the boys and girls ( want, wants ) to play two-square.

  B.   Everyone of the carpenters ( take, takes ) an afternoon break.

  C.   Neither his aunt nor his grandparents ( know, knows ) their departure time.

**PARTS OF SPEECH:   ADJECTIVES/ADVERBS**

  **Write a sentence using *hard* as an adjective:**

4.  A.   _____

  _____

  **Write a sentence using *hard* as an adverb:**

  B.   _____

  _____

**ANALOGIES:**

  **Circle the answer that best completes the analogy:**

5.  villi : intestines :: bronchi : _____
  (a) bronchitis      (b) esophagus      (c) lungs      (d) abdomen

**SENTENCE COMBINING:**

6.  John Carver was a rich man.
  He hired the ship for the Pilgrims' journey.
  He bought most of the goods for the Pilgrims' journey.

  _____

  _____

**DAY 178**

**CAPITALIZATION:**

1.  tomorrow, dad and lieut. lee will look for homes with the realtor from rainbow realty.

**PUNCTUATION:**

2.  A.  (magazine)  Time for Travel          F.  (album)  Cannon in D
    B.  (story)  Surprises in the Sea        G.  (poem)  At Woodward's Garden
    C.  (song)  Amazing Grace                H.  (play)  Junior Miss
    D.  (rhyme)  Mary Had a Little Lamb       I.  (book)  Symptoms
    E.  (newspaper)  City Tribune            J.  (magazine article)  America Style

**DICTIONARY:  GUIDE WORDS**
  Write <u>Yes</u> if the word could appear on the page with the following guide words;
  Write <u>No</u> if the word could not appear on that page:
       *brightness*          *brittle*

3.  A.  ____  bristle        C.  ____  brown       E.  ____  butter

    B.  ____  Brix Scale     D.  ____  brioche     F.  ____  Britain

**PARTS OF SPEECH:  CONJUNCTIONS**

4.  _____, _____, and _____ are the three most commonly used
    coordinating conjunctions.

**ANALOGIES:**

  **Circle the answer that best completes the analogy:**

5.  happy : jubilant :: threatening : _____
    (a) blackmail      (b) supportive      (c) resilient      (d) menacing

**SENTENCE COMBINING:**

6.  A wall must be built.
    A retaining one is needed.
    If not, the home might slide down the mountain.

    _____

    _____

**CAPITALIZATION:**

1.  the batu caves of kuala lampur, malaysia, house a hindu* shrine.

*world religion

**PUNCTUATION:**

2.  When Bob sailed on the Queen Elizabeth 2* to Europe he visited 10 Downing
    Street London England

*name of a ship

**SENTENCE TYPES:**

   **Write an interrogative sentence:**

3.  A.  _____

   **Write an imperative sentence:**

   B.  _____

**WORDS:**
  **Circle the correct word:**

4.  A.  ( Its, It's ) paw is caked with mud.
    B.  ( Your, You're ) required to have a physical to play sports, Thomas.
    C.  Because he is busy, we ( seldom, seldomly ) see him.
    D.  The fans cheered when ( their, there, they're ) team won.
    E.  The pianist played ( good, well ) at her first recital.
    F.  I don't feel ( good, well ).

**SENTENCES/FRAGMENTS/RUN-ONS:**
  **Write S for sentence, F for fragment, and R-O for run-on:**

5.  A.  ____  Until we agree.          C.  ____  I handed you a card look at it.

   B.  ____  He into the dumpster.   D.  ____  Take a few moments to decide.

**SENTENCE COMBINING:**

6.  James Oglethorpe started the colony of Georgia.
    He started the colony for poor people.
    He brought thirty families with him to America.

    _____

    _____

**DAY 180**

**CAPITALIZATION:**
  **Capitalize these titles:**

1.  A.  carmel, the little lost kitten

    B.  catch me if you can

    C.  "eat smart on the run"


**PUNCTUATION:**

2.  I believe  exclaimed Mr Tang  that the girls team has won by twenty two points


**PARTS OF SPEECH:   VERBS**
  **Underline the verb phrase twice:**

3.  A.  Your balloon has ( burst, busted ).
    B.  We should have ( brung, brought ) our swimming suits.
    C.  This dish must have ( broke, broken ) during shipping.
    D.  The papers are ( lying, laying ) on the coffee table.
    E.  Have you ( drank, drunk ) all the milk?


**PARTS OF SPEECH:   ADJECTIVES**
  **Circle any adjectives:**

4.  Many brave pioneers faced searing deserts and icy mountains to find a better life.


**ANALOGIES:**

  **Circle the answer that best completes the analogy:**

5.  praise : commend :: interrogate : _____
    (a) respond      (b) resuscitate      (c) degrade      (d) question


**SENTENCE COMBINING:**

6.  Harlem was first a Dutch settlement.
    It was started in 1653.
    It was named Nieuw Haarlem.

    _____

    _____

# Daily Grams:  Guided Review Aiding Mastery Skills – Grade 6

## ANSWERS

*AMV/RA:  Answers May Vary/Representative Answers     In sentence combining, other sentence structures are acceptable.*

**Day 1:**    **1.**  **T**ony, **I**, **S**panish, **U**ncle, **M**arco    **2.**  **T**ina, where's your six-speed bike?  **3.**  fierce (storm), tropical (storm)    **4.**  A. haven't   B. they're   C. isn't   D. I'll   E. don't   F. you're    **5. (b)** visualize    **6.**  AMV/RA:  These chocolate brownies have marshmallow on the inside.   These brownies with marshmallow on the inside are chocolate.

**Day 2:**    **1.**  **D**uring, **K**e'e, **B**each    **2.**  They'll swim, play games, and eat hot dogs at the party.    **3.**  in the garden; O. P. = garden    **4.**  AMV/RA:  twig, stadium  **5.**  A. <u>Syn.</u>   B. <u>Ant.</u>   C. <u>Syn.</u>   D. <u>Syn.</u>    **6.**  AMV/RA:  Both the first trolleys and first buses were drawn by horses.

**Day 3:**    **1.**  **T**he, **C**arr, **G**reenbriar, **R**oad, **W**ooley, **D**epartment, **S**tore    **2.**  No, I won't be there by 2 o'clock.    **3.**  A. declarative  B. interrogative    **4.**  ~~During the game~~, her <u>parents</u> <u>had cheered</u> loudly.    **5. (c)** state    **6.**  AMV/RA:  The white baby blanket has duck designs.  The baby blanket with duck designs is white.

**Day 4:**    **1.**  **W**e, **S**unday, **M**arch, **K**ansas, **J**emima    **2.**  The bus left on Thurs., May 9, 2001.    **3.**  A. child's toy   B. girls' puppy    **4.**  runs    **5.**  A. noted   B. locator   C. tasteless    **6.**  AMV/RA:  Their nephew is a goalie on a hockey team.   Their nephew who plays on a hockey team is a goalie.*

*Note:  If the clause is vital to the meaning of the sentence, commas are not used.

**Day 5:**    **1.**  **T**hey, **F**., **B**., **I**., **B**uilding, **W**hite, **H**ouse    **2.**  Linda said,  "We're eating soon."    **3.**  Tom and I    **4.**  A. <u>have ridden</u>   B. <u>was chosen</u>   C. <u>has lain</u>   D. <u>had brought</u>    **5.**  A. daring   B. debator   C. lonesome    **6.**  AMV/RA:  Professor Stein went to the Scottish island of Iona.   Professor Stein went to Iona, an island in Scotland.

**Day 6:**    **1.**  **H**as, **M**r., **D**avis, **S**t., **M**ary's, **H**ospital    **2.**  Let's go to the park, Andy.  **3.**  A. <u>C</u>   B. <u>C</u>   C. <u>P</u>   D. <u>P</u>   E. <u>P</u>   F. <u>C</u>    **4.**  A. Their (friends)   B. Two   C. You're    **5.**  A. <u>P</u>   B. <u>C</u>    **6.**  AMV/RA:  The hand has twenty-seven small bones that are moved by thirty-seven muscles.

**Day 7:**    **1.**  A. **H**ome, **R**ange   B. **L**ove, **Q**uestion    **2.**  His new address is 127 Low Dutch Road, Gettysburg, PA   17325.    **3.**  <u>I must have taken</u> a wrong turn.    **4.**  and, or    **5.**  A. <u>P</u>   B. <u>C</u>    **6.**  AMV/RA:  That girl, who attends my school, is selling cookies for a fund raiser.*   The girl who is selling cookies for a fund raiser attends my school.*

*Note: If the clause is vital to the meaning of the sentence, commas are not used. The significance of this clause is debatable; accept the sentence with or without commas.

**Day 8:**     1. Does, Jacy, East, Bellview, Avenue, Newport, Rhode, Island
2.   Barbara, my cousin, is a gymnast.  *or*  Barbara, my cousin is a gymnast.
3. AMV/RA: Whew!  Oops!     4. A. rugs   B. flashes   C. mice   D. houses
E. bays   F. stories     5. (d) meddler     6. AMV/RA:  Lani is reading while she is riding her exercise bike.

**Day 9:**     1. He, South, America, Freet, Middle, School     2. Did you, Mrs. Benson, find my notebook or language book?     3. The lady ~~with the poodle~~ is very funny.
4. A. AMV/RA: pause, halt     B. weight     C. AMV/RA: continue, proceed
5. A.  steaming     B. strained     C. redeemer     6. AMV/RA:  Clotted cream, also called Devonshire cream, is chiefly made in England.  Clotted or Devonshire cream is chiefly made in England.

**Day 10:**     1. Brad, I, Main, Street, Mayfest, Roxboro, North, Carolina     2. Yes, in fact, you're correct about that.     3. well     4. A. imperative   B. exclamatory
5. A. P   B. C     6. AMV/RA:  Stella bought an Arabian horse in Santa Fe last week.

**Day 11:**     1. Candace, A, Mojave, Desert     2. Miss Mary E. Ortiz works for Bart Co. in Tulsa, Oklahoma.     3. white (gown), embroidered (gown)     4. slowly, thoroughly
5. (a) offended     6. AMV/RA:  We bought the pine cupboard with glass doors at an auction.

**Day 12:**     1. The, Persian, Empire, B., C.     2. Nancy's guest list includes the following:  Mr. L. Sing, Dr. Lin Wong, and Mrs. Chika Cole.     3. A. present   B. future   C. past   4. and, but, or     5. A. Ant.   B. Syn.   C. Syn.   D. Ant.
6. AMV/RA:  A toad uses its sticky, forked tongue to capture insects.  A toad's sticky, forked tongue is used to capture insects.

**Day 13:**     1. A, Frenchman, Lafayette, America, Revolutionary, War     2. Rev. R.C. Collins, my minister, was born in Lake Wales, Florida.  *or*  Rev. R. C. Collins, my minister was born in Lake Wales, Florida.     3. a, an, the     4. under the earth
5. (d) generous     6. AMV/RA:  The ear is the organ of both hearing and balance. The ear is the organ of hearing and balance.

**Day 14:**
1.

> 12337 Clemmens Lane
> Fallbrook, CA  92028
> July 25, 2012

Dear Anne,
2. Nikko, weren't you born in Honolulu, Hawaii?     3. here, now, later     4. them
5. (c) deliberate     6. AMV/RA: After Kurt read the back of the cereal box, he put it into his cart.   Kurt read the back of the cereal box before putting it into his cart.

**Day 15:**    **1.** The, **U**., **S**., **C**apitol, **W**ashington, **D**., **C**., Union, Station    **2.** A. <u>The Black Stallion</u>   B. "Sunday for Sona"    **3.** A. yell, yells   B. break, breaks
**4.** he    **5.** A. losing   B. shameful   C. surely    **6.** AMV/RA: Danno is wearing a pinstriped suit for an interview.

**Day 16:**
**1.**   I.   Arizona cities
      **A.** Population under a million
      **B.** Population over a million
**2.** Their address is 4 Fordham Road, Tulsa, Oklahoma  74033.    **3.** During (During the storm), in (in August), of (of our trees), to (to the ground)    **4.** (a) dessert
(b) forest  (c) fruit  (d) garage  (e) hamlet    **5.** A.  manager   B.  managing
C.  management    **6.** AMV/RA: Kalingrad is an ice-free seaport located on the Baltic Sea.   Kalingrad, an ice-free seaport, is located on the Baltic Sea.   Located on the Baltic Sea, Kalingrad is an ice-free seaport.

**Day 17:**    **1.** In, **A**., **D**., Constantinople, Roman, Empire    **2.** The leader said, "That's a good idea, Sam."    **3.** there, together    **4.** Several <u>trucks</u> <u>were</u> already <u>loaded</u>.    **5.** A. <u>Ant</u>.   B. <u>Syn</u>.   C. <u>Syn</u>.   D. <u>Ant</u>.    **6.** AMV/RA:  Making a bed for her niece, Tara is sanding a log.

**Day 18:**    **1.** Their, **B**lue, **R**idge, **S**cenic, **R**ailway, **S**outh    **2.** Jacob's grandparents have given him twenty-one books.    **3.** tree, backyard, house    **4.** A. French   B. Swiss   C. Chinese   D. American    **5.** A. declaring  B. spiteful  C. announcement
D. precisely    **6.** AMV/RA:  After an armored car stopped in front of a jewelry store, the driver entered.

**Day 19:**
**1.**   The dinosaurs are not all dead.
    I saw one raise its iron head
    To watch me walking down the road
    Beyond our house today.
**2.** A. U. S.   B. bldg.   C. in.   D. Sen.    **3.** July (In July), camp (to a camp), group (with his church group)    **4.** A. they're   B. its   C. Your (button)    **5.** (d) genuine
**6.** AMV/RA:  The kitchen chair needs to be repaired because the back has fallen off.  Because the back has fallen off the kitchen chair, it needs to be repaired.

**Day 20:**    **1.** The, Garrison, Dam, Lake, Sakokawea, North, Dakota.    **2.** Three-fourths of Raymond's baseball cards aren't new.    **3.** <u>John</u> and <u>Holly</u> <u>mowed</u> the grass.    **4.** A.  sister's hamster   B.  sisters' hamster    **5.** A.  returnable   B.  ghostly
C.  thoughtful    **6.** AMV/RA:  Neither her first name nor her last name was spelled correctly.   Both her last and first names were misspelled.

**Day 21:**    **1.** Did, Captain, Christopher, Jones, Pilgrims, Mayflower    **2.** David said, "I can't go."    **3.** A.  not   B.  too   C.  very   D.  rather   E.  quite   F.  somewhat
G.  so    **4.** A. <u>could have swum</u>   B. <u>Has seen</u>   C. <u>must have drawn</u>   D. <u>was broken</u>
**5.** A.  locator   B.  bloated   C.  useful    **6.** AMV/RA:  Siamese cats have blue almond-

shaped eyes.

**Day 22:**   **1.** Alex, Did, Judaism   **2.** This steak, I think, is well-done.   **3.** A. <u>A</u>
B. <u>C</u>  C. <u>C</u>  D. <u>A</u>
**4.**
                                                        11 Coral Avenue
                                    **(A)**            Duluth, MN  55820
                                                        April 23, 20—
    **(C)**      Dear Patti,
    **(E)**                  We want to let you know we will be coming in July.
                             Our family plans to leave here after Independence Day!
                                    **(B)**                Your cousin,
                                    **(D)**                Carlos
**5.** (b) deduct   **6.** AMV/RA:  Tanning leather makes it stronger and more flexible.

**Day 23:**
**1.**
                                    5470 East Monroe Street
                                    Marathon, New York  13803
                                    January 15, 20—
        Dear Frank and Anna,
**2.** They're planning on ordering the following:  coke, pizza, and yogurt.   **3.** from my
aunt; O. P. = aunt   **4.** author, subject, title   **5.** (b) boredom   **6.** AMV/RA:
Cricket, a ball game, is played by two teams using flat bats.   Two teams use flat bats
when playing the ball game, cricket.

**Day 24:**   **1.** Joe, Juneau, Yukon, Territory, Evergreen, Cemetery   **2.** Two-fifths
of Brad's family should be arriving soon.   **3.** A. <u>Yes</u>  B. <u>No</u>  C. <u>No</u>  D. <u>Yes</u>
**4.** anybody   **5.** A. crusading  B. blameless  C. dependable   **6.** AMV/RA:
Faith rubbed her eyes because she was sleepy.   Sleepily, Faith rubbed her eyes.

**Day 25:**   **1.** Have, Molly, Cuyahoga, Valley, National, Recreation, Area
**2.** We're seeing the movie entitled <u>David and Goliath</u> today.   **3.** <u>One</u> ~~of the~~
~~raccoons~~ <u>waded</u> ~~across the street~~.   **4.** nonfiction   **5.** (a) affectionately
**6.** AMV/RA:  Jamaica, an island of the West Indies, is located south of Florida.
Jamaica, located south of Florida, is an island of the West Indies.

**Day 26:**   **1.** William, L., Shoemaker, Kentucky, Derbies   **2.** You're usually happy-
go-lucky and carefree.   **3.** A. don't  B. I'm  C. we're  D. can't  E. they've
F. they'll   **4.** harder   **5.** A. <u>P</u>  B. <u>C</u>   **6.** AMV/RA:  Bertie, my sister's
parakeet, likes to perch on my finger.

**Day 27:**   **1.** Do, German, Professor, Ritz, Miss, Lopez   **2.** A. <u>Roses for Mona</u>
B. "A Bird Came Walking down the Street"  C. "Every Dog Should Own a Man"
**3.** shiniest   **4.** <u>photographer</u> <u>took</u>; D. O. = picture   **5.** A. <u>C</u>  B. <u>P</u>   **6.** AMV/RA:
Give this note to the tall lady who is taking tickets.

**Day 28:**   **1.** Mr., Booth, North, American, Targo, Plant, Nursery   **2.** Her mother-in-
law was born on July 4, 1947.   **3.** A. girl's parakeet  B. girls' parakeet   **4.** atlas
**5.** A. matted  B. propped   C. sadness   **6.** AMV/RA:  Allison waved her hand

excitedly to hail a taxi and stepped into the street.   As Allison waved her hand excitedly to hail a taxi, she stepped into the street.

**Day 29:**   **1.** **M**ichael, **J**ordan, **C**hicago, **B**ulls, **N**ational, **B**asketball, **A**ssociation
**2.** Yeah!  Peter's uncle is coming!       **3.** he      **4.** at, until, above, from, before, except, in, for      **5.** A. stunning   B. smirked   C. scanner      **6.** AMV/RA:  Warm peach cobbler was served with vanilla ice cream.

**Day 30:**   **1.** **W**hen, **I**, **G**rammy, **R**emze, **I**, **L**eah      **2.** Please get the following change:  nickels, dimes, and quarters.       **3.** This (shirt), those (ones)      **4.** A. AMV/RA:  new, novel, young   B.  AMV/RA: antique, ancient      **5.** A. <u>F</u>   B. <u>S</u>
**6.** AMV/RA:  Although the brain weighs only three pounds, it has 400 thousand million nerve cells.

**Day 31:**   **1.** **J**oy, **N**ational, **A**ssociation, **M**anufacturers'      **2.** These houses, by the way, are small, secluded ones.      **3.** A. <u>RV</u>   B. <u>IV</u>   C. <u>RV</u>   D. <u>IV</u>   E. <u>RV</u>
F. <u>RV</u>      **4.** he      **5. (c)** criticism      **6.** AMV/RA:  Her favorite food is chicken marinated in mustard sauce.

**Day 32:**   **1.** **T**he, **Z**imbo, **R**estaurant, **C**restview, **A**venue, **S**outhern, **L**ouisiana
**2.** The newly-formed choir led by Mrs. Lewis sang "Home on the Range."*
**3.** hard, fast      **4.** A. <u>C</u>   B. <u>P</u>   C. <u>C</u>   D. <u>C</u>   E. <u>C</u>   F. <u>P</u>      **5.** A. gazing
B. stranded   C. strapped      **6.** AMV/RA:  Hunting for his missing shoe, he found a five dollar bill.  He found a five dollar bill while hunting for his missing shoe.

*Note:  Also accept commas before and after *led by Mrs. Lewis.*

**Day 33:**   **1.** **T**hey, **D**avis, **C**reek, **R**eservoir, **O**rd, **N**ebraska      **2.** Mike, do you take swimming lessons at the Y.M.C.A.*?      **3.** A. imperative   B. declarative   C. exclamatory      **4.** work      **5. (c)** ascend      **6.** AMV/RA:  After the first grader sounded out a word, he (she) smiled at his (her) father.

Note:  Some texts teach that this abbreviation may also appear without periods.

**Day 34:**   **1.** **O**n, **St.**, **P**atrick's, **D**ay, **P**aul, **R**oute, **M**alheur, **N**ational, **W**ildlife, **R**efuge
**2.** Ms. Diaz, is the ladies' bowling team competing today?      **3.** A. <u>C</u>   B. <u>A</u>   C. <u>A</u>
D. <u>C</u>   E. <u>C</u>   F. <u>A</u>      **4.** well      **5.** A. priceless   B. pitted   C. relieving
**6.** AMV/RA:  Vikings launched raids in longboats which had one row of oars on each side.  Longboats used by the Vikings to launch raids had one row of oars on each side.

**Day 35:**   **1.** **T**y, **C**obb, **N**ational, **B**aseball, **H**all, **F**ame      **2.** The boys' club will meet at 5:30 P. M.* on Monday, June 5<sup>th</sup>.      **3.** A. storms   B. men   C. tables   D. ditches
E. speeches   F. deer      **4.** A. scare(s), scared   B. follow(s), followed   C. eat(s), ate      **5. (d)** giver      **6.** AMV/RA:  The English sparrow was introduced into the United States to fight cankerworms.

*Note:  Some texts teach that this may appear without periods and with lower case letters.

**Day 36:**    **1. T**he, **S**traban, **T**ownship, **C**hambersburg, **P**ike
**2.** Dear Deka,

      Bring your new blue dress with you.

          Love,
          Sally

**3.** up, down    **4.** electrician, light, garage    **5.** AMV/RA: jewelry    **6.** AMV/RA: Large red bows were attached to the collected stuffed bears; they were then donated to a children's hospital.   After stuffed bears were collected and large red bows attached, they were donated to a children's hospital.

**Day 37:**
**1.    M**usic, when soft voices die,
    **V**ibrates in the memory--
**2.** This half-filled balloon, most certainly, needs more air, Micah.    **3.** from, of, with, across, beyond, after, in, off    **4.** (a) mental   (b) metal   (c) nearby   (d) sack   (e) sea   (f) system    **5.** AMV/RA: hockey, volleyball, soccer    **6.** AMV/RA: Because warfare was common in Europe during the Middle Ages, castles were built for protection.

**Day 38:**    **1. A**fter, **R**ubio's, **D**epartment, **S**tore, **M**om, **G**reenbelt, **P**ark    **2.** Roy said, "I've lost my keys and my wallet."    **3.** A.  decide(s), decided   B.  run(s), ran   C.  see(s), saw   D.  play(s), played    **4.** A.  a, an, the   B.  this, that, those, these
**5. (a)** shorten    **6.** AMV/RA:  Melissa likes to read mysteries, but Carli likes to read science fiction.

**Day 39:**    **1. A, B**aptist, **C**hristian, **F**ebruary    **2.** The children's playground is located at 27 Swan Drive, Hillsborough, NC  27278.    **3.** we    **4.** A. P̲  B. C̲
**5.** A. dimly   B.  scarred   C. reaction    **6.** AMV/RA:  Magpies are scavengers that often collect small, bright objects.   Magpies, scavengers, often collect small, bright objects.

**Day 40:**    **1. D**r., **P**arks, **D**ad, **L**emon, **T**ree, **G**olf, **C**lub, **M**emorial, **D**ay    **2.** A. Exercise World̲̲   B.  "How to Play Outfield"   C.  Gold Rush Prodigal̲    **3.** The rodeo cowboy̲ lassoed̲ the steer and quickly tied̲ it.    **4.** AMV/RA: thesaurus
**5. (b)** grizzly    **6.** AMV/RA:  When we called our grandmother, she was painting her house.

**Day 41:**    **1. H**ave, **M**om, **M**ajesty, **T**ower, **G**ardens, **F**lorida
**2.**  I.  Literature
      **A.**   Prose
         1.   Plays
         2.   Novels
      **B.**   Poetry
**3.** very, rather    **4.** done    **5. (c)** wall    **6.** AMV/RA:  They laid tile in their entryway, carpeting in their living room, and linoleum in their kitchen.

**Day 42:**   **1.** A, Sierra, Madre, Mountains, West   **2.** Have Mrs. Minter and Capt. Brewer presented an award to the city's mayor?   **3.** Yippee!   **4.** them
**5. (b)** corduroy   **6.** AMV/RA: All three species of kiwi birds are protected.

**Day 43:**   **1.** Naomi, Are, Antarctica   **2.** Jan Clark, D.D.S., can't be here today.
**3.** bag (with his bag), street (into the street)   **4.** A. doesn't   B. she's   C. I'll
D. they're   E. hadn't   F. here's   **5.** A. foolish   B. gnashed   C. degrading
D. slatted   **6.** AMV/RA: The father rocked the baby as he sang to him (her).

**Day 44:**   **1.** Was, R., M., S., Titanic, Belfast, Ireland   **2.** That small, chubby baby
won't come to me.   **3.** often, never   **4.** At the picnic, some people were playing
volleyball.   **5.** A. steadied   B. steadies   C. steadying   **6.** AMV/RA: Although
the child was dirty from playing in the dirt, she did not want to take a bath.

**Day 45:**   **1.** In, Kiwanis, Club, Abbeville-Greenwood, Regional, Library
**2.**                       Ms. Sarah I. Thorpe
                             5712 E. Penny Lane
                             Tacoma, WA   98408
**3.** A. C   B. A   C. A   D. C   E. C   F. A   **4.** A. Japanese   B. Franklin
C. English   **5.** A. DC   B. IC   **6.** AMV/RA: The round window in the hallway has
roses on it.   The hallway window is round with roses on it.

**Day 46:**   **1.** The, OSHA, Department, Labor   **2.** Yes, my grandpa, Julian S. Rios,
lives nearby.   **3.** but   **4.** (C) heading   (D) salutation (greeting)   (A) body   (E) closing
(B) signature   **5.** A. hasty   B. hurting   C. stirred   **6.** AMV/RA: A potto is an
African animal with wooly fur.   A potto, an animal with wooly fur, lives in Africa.

**Day 47:**   **1.** The, Asia   **2.** If you aren't going, let's play table tennis.   **3.** most
quickly   **4.** almanac   **5. (a)** fan   **6.** AMV/RA: Emma is a lawyer who wants to
have her own law firm.   Emma, a lawyer, wants to have her own law firm.

**Day 48:**   **1.** After, St., Paul's, Cathedral, London, Hyde, Park   **2.** In the car, seat
yourself by the back window.   **3.** better   **4.** Miss Valentino and her grandmother
have arrived at the airport.   **5.** A. receiving   B. batter   C. tasteful   **6.** AMV/RA:
The circus is coming to town, but I cannot attend.

**Day 49:**   **1.** The, Doha, Persian, Gulf, Arabia   **2.** Shawn graduated in '92 in
Hanover, Pennsylvania.   **3.** Recently, downtown   **4.** A. No   B. No   C. No   D.
Yes   **5.** A. reclusive   B. wrapped   C. dented   **6.** AMV/RA: In 1913, Hudson
Stuck was the first to climb Alaska's Mt. McKinley.

**Day 50:**   **1.** The, Federalist, Party, Alexander, Hamilton   **2.** A. Island of the Blue
Dolphins   B. My Side of the Mountain   C. Animal Journal   D. "Seven Ways to Help
Your Child"   **3.** A. Yes   B. No   C. No   D. Yes   E. Yes   F. Yes   **4.** A.
AMV/RA: stable   B. strait   C. AMV/RA: use, eat   **5. (a)** gate   **6.** AMV/RA:
Kami is wrapping her dishes in newspaper and placing them in a moving box.

**Day 51:**   **1.** The, Pebble, Shoe, Co., Royal, Street
**2.**
12 West Palm Lane
Burger, TX  79007
April 9, 20—

Dear Stan,

**3.** fiction    **4.** A. woman's truck  B. boys' club  C. children's shoes    **5.** A. donkeys  B. relayed  C. denied    **6.** AMV/RA:  Ravens can be found in the icy Arctic and in the warm regions of the Northern Hemisphere.

**Day 52:**   **1.** Will, Animal, Welfare, League, Phoenix, Civic, Plaza, Adams, Street, Dee    **2.** Rick, dot your i in the first word of your paragraph.    **3.** A. too  B. You're  C. There    **4.** **fewer** points (Box *points*.)    **5.** A. F̲  B. S̲    **6.** AMV/RA:  As the carpenter picked up lumber, he turned to talk to the foreman.

**Day 53:**   **1.** On, Saturday, Dad, Brighton, Bakery, Regal, Avenue    **2.** A. mts.  B. Tues.  C. co.  D. B.C.  E. Aug.  F. blvd.    **3.** she    **4.** well    **5. (d)** submerge    **6.** AMV/RA:  Mr. Ving returns all phone calls every day after he eats lunch.

**Day 54:**   **1.** Does, Luana, Beach, Resort, Hotel, Russian    **2.** He was born on Thurs., Mar. 26, 1992, in Miami, Florida.    **3.** A̲r̲e̲ the c̲u̲p̲s̲ and s̲a̲u̲c̲e̲r̲s̲    **4.** A. AMV/RA: bear, bolt  B. AMV/RA: Mt. Elden, Laylah    **5.** A. bullied  B. graceful  C. residing    **6.** AMV/RA:  Lungfish live in the rivers of South America, Africa, and Australia.

**Day 55:**   **1.** The, Olympic, Games, Rome, B., C.    **2.** A. M̲o̲r̲n̲i̲n̲g̲ ̲T̲r̲i̲b̲u̲n̲e̲  B. "Westward Expansion"  C. "Winter Wonderland"  D. T̲r̲a̲v̲e̲l̲ ̲D̲e̲l̲i̲g̲h̲t̲    **3.** A. interrogative  B. imperative  C. declarative    **4.** A. I̲V̲  B. R̲V̲  C. R̲V̲  D. I̲V̲  E. I̲V̲  F. I̲V̲    **5. (a)** flower    **6.** AMV/RA:  The newborn colt shakily struggled to its feet.

**Day 56:**   **1.** Many, Panama, Canal
**2.**
37 Osborn Road
San Antonio, TX  79007
Dec. 27, 20—

Dear Luana,

Your aunt,
Chessa

**3. (a)** cord  **(b)** east  **(c)** egg  **(d)** elegant  **(e)** float  **(f)** harbor    **4.** raceway, cars, line, time    **5. (b)** egg    **6.** AMV/RA:  Carlo usually takes out the garbage before going to bed at midnight.   After taking out the garbage at midnight, Carlo usually goes to bed.

**Day 57:**   **1.** The, U., S., Department, Health, Human, Services    **2.** Their boys' club is at 212 Fee Street, Bend, Oregon 97702.    **3.** A. ovens  B. boys  C. babies  D. mice  E. moose  F. halves    **4.** O̲n̲e̲ of the magazines i̲s̲ on the table.    **5.** A. precisely  B. dreading  C. desirous    **6.** AMV/RA:  That old barn is used to store farm equipment.   That barn which is used to store farm equipment is old.

**Day 58:**　**1.** In, Roman, Catholic, Eastern　**2.** On July 4, 1776, America's independence was declared.

**3.**

| along | below | out | concerning | doubt | inside | through | up |
|---|---|---|---|---|---|---|---|
| within | or | my | regarding | since | beside | belong | no |
| past | too | down | against | toward | into | himself | in |

**4.** doesn't　**5.** A. S　B. F　**6.** AMV/RA: Tourism, oil refining, and financial dealings make the country of Aruba prosper.


**Day 59:**

**1.**　I.　Flying insects
　　A.　Harmful ones
　　　　1. Insects that spread diseases
　　　　2. Poisonous insects
　　B.　Harmless ones

**2.** Towels, shirts, and pants lay in a knee-deep heap on the floor.　**3.** A. AMV/RA: going away from the normal route　B. tour　**4.** upstream　**5.** A. inventive B. pastries　C. volleys　**6.** AMV/RA: The doctor placed eight stitches in her hand and explained caring for them.　After the doctor put eight stitches in her hand, he (she) explained how to care for the stitches.


**Day 60:**　**1.** The, Brawner, Strawberry, Folk, Festival, South　**2.** J. F. Kennedy was assassinated in Dallas, Texas, on November 22, 1963.　**3.** long (hair), brown (hair), gentle (breeze)　**4.** should have thrown　**5.** (a) soothe　**6.** AMV/RA: Charles M. Schulz was an American cartoonist who created the Peanuts comic strip.　Charles M. Schulz, an American cartoonist, created the Peanuts comic strip.


**Day 61:**

**1.**
　　　　　　　　　　　　　　　　7891 West Crocus Drive
　　　　　　　　　　　　　　　　Mission Viejo, CA　92692
　　　　　　　　　　　　　　　　Jan. 31, 20—

　　Dear Aunt Grace,

　　　　　　　　　　　　　　　　Sincerely yours,
　　　　　　　　　　　　　　　　Wilma

**2.** The short, funny lady bought twenty-seven balloons for the party.　**3.** A. will or shall seem　B. will or shall fall　**4.** us　**5.** (d) handle　**6.** AMV/RA: Mahogany is a hard wood that resists termites.　Mahogany, a hard wood, resists termites.


**Day 62:**　**1.** Their, Iceland, Vatnajokull, Europe　**2.** You, without a doubt, don't want this half-eaten sandwich.　**3.** whom　**4.** An army ~~of ants~~ marched silently ~~across the brick walkway~~.　**5.** A. Ant.　B. Ant.　C. Syn.　**6.** AMV/RA: The antique plate with gold trim has a small pink rose in its center.　The gold-trimmed plate with a small rose on its center is antique.


**Day 63:**　**1.** Was, Sarah, Caldwell, Metropolitan, Opera　**2.** A. Sun.　B. Mon. C. Tues.　D. Wed.　E. Thurs.　F. Fri.　G. Sat.　**3.** me, him, her, it, you, them, us, whom　**4.** not, too　**5.** A. DC　B. IC　**6.** AMV/RA: Balsamic vinegar which is an aged Italian vinegar is made from the must of white grapes.   Balsamic vinegar, an aged Italian vinegar, is made from the must of white grapes.

**Day 64:**     **1. P**ets, **P**acific, **C**rest, **T**rail, **N**orth, **C**ascades, **N**ational, **P**ark
**2.** A. Jan.  B. Feb.  C. Mar.  D. Apr.  E. May  F. June  G. July  H. Aug.
I. Sept.  J. Oct.  K. Nov.  L. Dec.     **3.**  A <u>nurse</u> <u>studied</u> the chart and <u>talked</u> <s>to the patient</s>.     **4.** A. author, subject, title   B. This refers to children's literature.
**5.** A. whistling  B. fenced  C. resourceful    **6.** AMV/RA:  Whereas Pierre likes to scuba dive, his sister likes to snorkel.   Pierre likes to scuba dive; his sister likes to snorkel.

**Day 65:**     **1. D**id, **G**eronimo, **C**hiricahua, **A**pache, **P**resident, **T**eddy, **R**oosevelt
**2.** "You're extremely efficient," said Mr. Elton to the mechanic.     **3.** carefully, fast
**4.** me    **5.** A. bubbling  B. responsive  C. reprisal    **6.** AMV/RA:  The little girl is helping her aunt to plant a garden by placing water in each hole.   Placing water in each hole, the little girl is helping her aunt to plant a garden.

**Day 66:**     **1. T**he, **M**iddle, **A**ges
**2.** Mentor Company, Inc.
       24 Zuni Hills Rd.
       Sonoma, CA   95370

       Ladies and Gentlemen of the Board:
**3.** A. <u>N</u>  B. <u>A</u>    **4.** most strangely    **5.** (a) watercolor    **6.** AMV/RA:  Although the ermine is called a short-tailed weasel in North America, it was called a stoat in the Old World.

**Day 67:**     **1.** A. **C**loud, **J**ewel  B. **A**, **D**utch, **P**icture   C. **L**ove, **F**inds, **H**ome
**2.** Yeah!  We're leaving on the <u>Super Chief</u>, a famous train.     **3.** has    **4.** A. I'll
B. won't  C. we're  D. it's  E. haven't  F. there's    **5.** A. <u>P</u>  B. <u>C</u>
**6.** AMV/RA:  Before Lauren leaves for work at six each morning, she packs a lunch.

**Day 68:**     **1.** In, **B**ritish, **G**ulf, **M**exico, **N**ew, **O**rleans    **2.** My sister-in-law and Miss Gorham introduced us to Nancy Reese, a newspaper reporter.     **3.** AMV/RA:  Ugh! This tastes terrible!    **4.** Columbian, British    **5.** A. <u>DC</u>  B. <u>IC</u>    **6.** AMV/RA:  The blooming tree is filled with fragrant white blossoms.*   Filled with white fragrant blossoms, the tree is blooming.*

*Note:  No comma is needed between two descriptive adjectives if one is a color.

**Day 69:**     **1. T**he, **H**an, **G**ou, **C**anal, **C**hi, **B**ejing    **2.** A. <u>Silver Express</u>  B. <u>Rural Life</u>   C. "Phoning Home"  D. <u>Collected Poems</u>  E. "Travel"    **3.** and, but, or
**4.** (a) oboe  (b) obtain  (c) permit  (d) prince  (e) print  (f) prior    **5.** A. positively
B. huffiest  C. trendy    **6.** AMV/RA:  Bobsledding has been an Olympic event since 1924 when the first Winter Games were held.

**Day 70:**   **1.** The, Japanese, **Shinkansen**   **2.** Brett, your two sons' stained, striped shirts can't be washed.   **3.** A. <u>C</u>  B. <u>A</u>  C. <u>A</u>  D. <u>C</u>  E. <u>C</u>  F. <u>C</u>
**4.** magazines   **5. (d)** warning   **6.** AMV/RA:  His grandfather's friend who was in the U. S. Army during World War II was part of the Normandy Invasion.

**Day 71:**   **1.** **W**alter, **P**erry, **J**ohnson, **W**ashington, **S**enators   **2.** On Friday, May 27, 2012, his class will be graduating.   **3.** A. <u>S</u>  B. <u>F</u>  C. <u>F</u>   **4.** biographical
**5.** A. unseemly  B. horrified   C. horrifying   **6.** AMV/RA:  The end of a nerve cell or axon sends impulses to other cells.  The end of a nerve cell, an axon, sends impulses to other cells.

**Day 72:**   **1.** Did, Hiawatha, National, Forest, Great, Lakes   **2.** No, I'm not upset, disturbed, or angry.   **3.** A. <u>has risen</u>  B. <u>was lying</u>  C. <u>could have set</u>   **4. (E)** heading (C) salutation (greeting) (A) body (B) closing (D) signature   **5. (a)** direction
**6.** AMV/RA:  The small apartment on the third floor is perfect for the young couple.

**Day 73:**   **1.** Developed, German, Louis, Doberman, Doberman   **2.** The A. M. A. held a doctors' conference at 6:30 P.M.   **3.** well   **4.** A. Their (basket)   B. Its (tail)   C. We're   D. your (shoes)   **5.** A. <u>DC</u>  B. <u>IC</u>   **6.** AMV/RA:  Zane Gray was an American writer who wrote mostly about the West.

**Day 74:**   **1.** Did, Grandfather, Mellon, Leave, It, Beaver   **2.** Is that four-poster bed from the movie set of <u>Gone with the Wind</u>?   **3.** The <u>banker</u> ~~in the blue suit~~ <u>may have</u> <u>spoken</u> ~~to my grandmother's club~~.   **4.** A. present  B. future  C. past
**5.** A. leisurely  B. ripped   C. glorious   **6.** AMV/RA:  Whistling loudly, the impatient father tried to get his son's attention.   The impatient father who tried to get his son's attention whistled loudly.

**Day 75:**   **1.** The, Protestant, Rabbi, Greene   **2.** A garter snake, he believes, isn't very scary.   **3.** they   **4.** A. like  B. meows   **5.** A. <u>IC</u>  B. <u>DC</u>
**6.** AMV/RA:  Charles Peale painted portraits of George Washington, Thomas Jefferson, Alexander Hamilton, and John Adams.

**Day 76:**   **1.** During, Space, Age, Neil, Armstrong   **2.** A. <u>Seas and Seashells</u>
B. "West Indies Map"   C. "The Necklace"   D. <u>Herbie Rides Again</u>   **3.** any
**4.** A. rail   B. one track or a vehicle on one track   C. cycle   D. 2   **5.** A.  removal
B. satisfied  C. satisfying   **6.** AMV/RA:  When a young woman stepped off the train filled with tourists, she twisted her ankle.  As a young woman stepped off the tourist-filled train, she twisted her ankle.

**Day 77:**   **1.** Due, Grandpa, Renicki, Plumbing   **2.** A recipe for creamy, spiced sauce was written in <u>Food and Fashion</u>.   **3.** A. you'll   B. where's  C. don't
D. I'm  E. haven't  F. I'd   **4.** A. interrogative   B. exclamatory  C. imperative
**5. (b)** tree   **6.** AMV/RA:  You must take a number at that deli, or you won't be served.  In order to be served at that deli, you must take a number.

**Day 78:**   **1.** Spencer, Tracey, Academy, Award, Captain, Courageous
**2.**

                                      11260 N. 58th Ave.
                                      Glendale, AZ 85306
                                      Feb. 1, 20—

     Dear Koko,
          You're one of my favorite cousins. Let's go to the zoo next week.
                             Love,
                             Chandra
                    **D.O.**

**3.** he   **4.** The little <u>boy</u> <u>cuddled</u> a puppy ~~in his arms~~.   **5.** A. allowed   B. markers
C. currently   **6.** AMV/RA: The pea-sized pineal gland is located at the base of the brain.

**Day 79:**   **1.** A, Trend, Travel, Queen, Victoria's, Ireland   **2.** My neighbor likes to watch <u>Jeopardy</u> and to read short, romantic novels.   **3.** A. feet   B. buzzes   C. alleys   D. proofs   E. secretaries   F. pleas   **4.** slowly   **5. (d)** scrutinize
**6.** AMV/RA: Because Lisa's grandpa has to work, he can't attend her softball game.

**Day 80:**   **1.** The, U., S., Marine, Silent, Drill, Team, Arlington, National, Cemetery
**2.**   Cardon Co.
    2742 E. Lewis Street
    Kansas City, MO 64111

    Dear Sir:
**3.** A. <u>**may be** going</u>   B. <u>**could have** gone</u>   C. <u>**has** made</u>   **4.** crystal (vase), silky (roses), pink (roses), glass (marbles)   **5.** A. global   B. porous   C. crazily
**6.** AMV/RA: Marco is a mechanic who works on foreign cars at Euro Car Repair.

**Day 81:**   **1.** Mt., Olympus, Sol, Duc, Hot, Springs, Washington   **2.** Sharon, my cousin, lives in Kosciusko, Mississippi.   or   Sharon, my cousin lives in Kosciusko, Mississippi.   **3.** us   **4.** (a) less  (b) light  (c) lipid  (d) lips  (e) rust  (f) rustler
**5.** A. ✔   B. __   C. ✔   **6.** AMV/RA: Having had a tonsillectomy, Mario is in St. Andrew's Hospital.   Mario is in St. Andrew's Hospital because he has had a tonsillectomy.

**Day 82:**   **1.** Today's, Casper, Wyoming, Oregon, Trail, Pony, Express
**2.** Mrs. Schwartz, may I read this article entitled "Minnesota Draws Tourists" for my current events paper?   **3.** A. <u>RV</u>  B. <u>RV</u>  C. <u>IV</u>  D. <u>IV</u>  E. <u>IV</u>  F. <u>RV</u>   **4.** The <u>fans</u> ~~in the first row~~ and the <u>ushers</u> <u>applauded</u> loudly.   **5. (c)** pledge   **6.** AMV/RA: Although Will is only sixteen years old, he is nearly as tall as his father.

**Day 83:**   **1.** A. Sand, Dunes   B. Incident, French, Camp   C. My, Life, Big, Cats
**2.** When you're upset, it's a good idea to count to ten, Wendy.   **3.** (You) <u>stay</u>
**4.** more colorful   **5.** A. <u>IC</u>  B. <u>DC</u>   **6.** AMV/RA: Pia's mother crocheted the white lacy tablecloth with red rosebuds.   The white lacy tablecloth with red rosebuds was crocheted by Pia's mother.

**Day 84:**

**1.**

555 Maple Lane
Hanover, NJ 07936
August 1, 2001

Dear Lani,

Sincerely,
Mary

**2.** Don't we need the following: lettuce, tomatoes, and cucumbers?    **3.** We
**4.** A. <u>No</u>  B. <u>No</u>  C. <u>Yes</u>  D. <u>No</u>  E. <u>Yes</u>  F. <u>Yes</u>    **5.** (c) pounding
**6.** AMV/RA:  The couple bought a vine-covered cottage on a lake.

**Day 85:    1.** The, Fantasy, Island, Wailua, Falls, Hawaii    **2.** The babies' diapers
aren't paper; they're cloth.    **3.** AMV/RA:  <u>Phew</u>! That smells strong!    **4.** A. <u>P</u>
B. <u>P</u>  C. <u>C</u>  D. <u>C</u>    **5.** A. belittling  B. frayed  C. dryness    **6.** AMV/RA:
Joshua lifted his niece, kissed her, and placed her in a highchair.  Lifting his niece,
Joshua kissed her before placing her in a highchair.

**Day 86:    1.** Is, Harvard, Center, Risk, Analysis, U., S., D., A., Senator, Togas
**2.** Hurrah! One-half of the players on our team will be stars!    **3.** A. <u>A</u>  B. <u>N</u>
**4.** Dad, bus, town    **5.** (b) sleepily    **6.** AMV/RA:  Alec enjoys his detective work
for the Mirage Police Department.

**Day 87:    1.** Cole, Julio, I, Woodrow, Mall, Interstate, Toledo    **2.** His company's
president flew on the <u>Concartia</u>.    **3.** nonfiction    **4.** A. AMV/RA: counterfeit
B. AMV/RA: through   C. AMV/RA: real, authentic    **5.** A. <u>F</u>  B. <u>F</u>    **6.** AMV/RA:
Neil made scrambled eggs, French toast, and cherry fritters for lunch.

**Day 88:    1.** We, Natchez, Trace, Parkway, Native, American    **2.** A. <u>Four
Seasons</u>  B. "In the Garden"   C. "Little Miss Muffet"   D. "The Apprentice"   E.
<u>Parents</u>  F. <u>Comedy in Como</u>    **3.** and, or    **4.** AMV/RA:  A. Danube River
B. Harvey Jones  C. Cardinals  D. Starburst Nursery    **5.** (b) transparent
**6.** AMV/RA:  Watching a funny movie, the teenagers laughed.  When the teenagers
watched a funny movie, they laughed.

**Day 89:    1.** His, In, U., S., Lighthouse, Society    **2.** A sun-bleached, artificial plant
was discarded.
**3.**  least      perhaps    **below**    **down**     **for**     **into**     here      **until**     **from**
     **within**   **throughout** **across**    soon     **by**     again     need     **except**    his
**4.** A. Mrs. James's notebook    B. women's company    C. Aaron and Victor's blocks
**5.** A. beautiful  B. carrier  C. baggage    **6.** AMV/RA:  Maria watched a
championship basketball game on television before going to the library.  After Maria
watched a championship game on television, she went to the library.

**Day 90:    1.** The, Mill, Mountain, Zoo, Groundhog, Day    **2.** A. Sun.  B. Mon.  C.
Tues.  D. Wed.  E. Thurs.  F. Fri.  G. Sat.    **3.** A. <u>F</u>   B. <u>F</u>  C. <u>S</u>    **4.** a, an,
the    **5.** A. shunned  B. cantoring  C. sloppiness    **6.** AMV/RA:  McKinley

National Park in Alaska was renamed Denali National Park in 1980.  Alaska's McKinley National Park was renamed Denali National Park in 1980.

**Day 91:    1. G**rammy, **K**uykendall, **R**ebox, **N**ews, **D**utch
**2.**  I.  Artists
    A.  Impressionistic artists
        1.  American
        2.  European
           a.  Manet
           b.  Renoir
    B.  Surrealistic artists
**3.** A. <u>L</u>   B. <u>A</u>    **4.** black    **5.** A. <u>IC</u>  B. <u>DC</u>    **6.** AMV/RA:  Idaho is bordered by six Western states and the Canadian province of British Columbia.

**Day 92:    1. T**he, **G**erman, **C**ooking 101    **2.** A. Jan.   B. Feb.   C. Mar.   D. Apr.   E. May   F. June   G. July   H. Aug.   I. Sept.   J. Oct.   K. Nov.   L. Dec.
**3.** A. <u>A</u>  B. <u>P</u>    **4.** infinitive    **5. (c)** kidnap    **6.** AMV/RA:  Labor Day, which is a holiday in the United States and Canada, honors the laborer.*

*Note:  One may debate using commas before and after the clause, *which is a holiday in the United States and Canada.*  If the clause is considered vital to the sentence, commas are not used.  You might want to discuss this with students.

**Day 93:    1.** A. **B**eautiful, **D**reamer  B. **S**taking, **H**er, **C**laim    C. **H**ow, **D**o, **I**, **L**ove, **T**hee    **2.**  Japanese Flower Co.
       456 N. Ukiah Pl.
       Kokomo, IN   46902

       Dear Mr. Yakimoto:
**3.**  A. They're  B. Your (face)  C. doesn't    **4.** Sir Francis Drake, Englishman, San Francisco Bay    **5. (d)** exposed    **6.** AMV/RA:  Ramona found a velvet sack containing several gold coins in an old chest.   Ramona found several gold coins in a velvet sack within an old chest.

**Day 94:    1. I**n, **R**oss, **P**alomar, **C**ollege, **C**alifornia.
**2.**    Dear Alice,
      Mindy's father-in-law was born in Alabaster, Alabama, on September 23,
    1952. Will this information help you to write your business report?
                                 Always,
                                 Dean
**3.** <u>s</u>, <u>sh</u>, <u>ch</u>, <u>x</u>, <u>z</u>    **4.** better    **5.** A. reprimanding   B. centuries   C. responsive
**6.** AMV/RA:  The Pyrenees Mountains separating Spain from France are rich in timber.  Rich in timber, the Pyreness Mountains separate Spain and France.

**Day 95:    1. T**he, **A**tlantic, **O**cean, **M**editerranean, **S**ea, **A**frica    **2.** The group held a meeting in Dallas, Texas, last winter – odd time for golfers.  *or* (odd time for golfers)
**3.** A. has or have gone  B. had gone    **4.** <u>Haven</u>'t <u>you</u> <u>finished</u> the ironing?
**5. (b)** England    **6.** AMV/RA:  Susie bought Adirondack chairs for the patio at Today's Outdoor Store.

**Day 96:**    **1. R**are, **S**epilok, **S**anctuary, **B**orneo    **2.** These four may go: Dawn, Christy, Jacob, and Tate.    **3.** abstract    **4.** cat    **5. A.** startling   **B.** strapped   **C.** insurance    **6.** AMV/RA:  The man smiled as he placed an engagement ring on a dessert plate.   Placing an engagement ring on a dessert plate, the man smiled.

**Day 97:**    **1. H**is, **D**ogwood, **M**edical, **C**linic, **G**eorgia    **2.** "Their team's final score was twenty-seven points," said Cole.    **3.** lawyer    **4. A.** <u>P</u>   **B.** <u>P</u>   **C.** <u>C</u>   **5. (c)** Washington Monument    **6.** AMV/RA:  The Women's Army Corp was formed in 1942 after the United States entered World War II.

**Day 98:**    **1. A. G**irl, **D**ream   **B. T**he, **N**ight, **T**hey, **B**urned, **M**ountain   **C. A**n, **O**ld, **W**oman, **R**oads    **2.** Eli said, "Go east on Bear Blvd. until you come to a Y-shaped street."   **3.** geographical    **4.** I    **5. A.** debatable   **B.** changeable   **C.** erasable    **6.** AMV/RA:  His favorite pants are covered with paint, but he continues to wear them.

**Day 99:**    **1. O**n, **N**ovember, **A**rmistice, **D**ay, **W**orld, **W**ar    **2. A.** <u>Valley Independent</u>   **B.** "Celebrations"   **C.** <u>Eleanor</u>   **D.** "A Dutch Picture"    **3. (a)** idea   **(b)** jeep   **(c)** jest   **(d)** knack   **(e)** know   **(f)** koala    **4. A.** <u>A</u>   **B.** <u>N</u>   **C. A** <u>N</u>   **D.** <u>N</u>    **5. A.** <u>IC</u>   **B.** <u>DC</u>    **6.** AMV/RA:  They needed sheets for a king-size bed, but they bought sheets for a queen-size bed.   Although they needed sheets for a king-size bed, they bought sheets for a queen-size bed.

**Day 100:**    **1. T**he, **H**imalaya, **M**ountains, **A**sia, **I**ndia    **2.** A tall, handsome cowboy, a rodeo star, left for Billings, Montana.    **3. A.** she's   **B.** we're   **C.** can't   **D.** didn't   **E.** they'll   **F.** shouldn't   **G.** hasn't   **H.** won't   **I.** I've    **4. A.** imperative   **B.** exclamatory   **C.** declarative   **D.** interrogative    **5. A.** <u>IC</u> **B.** <u>DC</u>    **6.** AMV/RA:  Cos lettuce, also called romaine lettuce, can withstand heat better than other lettuces.   Cos or romaine lettuce can withstand heat better than other lettuces.

**Day 101:**    **1. W**e, **H**osewell, **P**lantation, **T**homas, **L**ynch, **J**r., **D**eclaration, Independence    **2.** On Tuesday, July 3, 1992, we went camping in Bangor, Maine.   **3. A.** <u>must have brought</u>   **B.** <u>Should have taken</u>   **C.** <u>may have gone</u>   **D.** <u>had drunk</u>   **4.** Later, everywhere, rather    **5. (d)** honesty    **6.** AMV/RA:  The child, refusing to cooperate, sat on a chair and pouted.   The child who refused to cooperate sat on a chair and pouted.   Sitting on a chair and pouting, the child refused to cooperate.

**Day 102:**    **1. M**iss, **A**rter, **C**anadian, **L**ogan, **J**unior, **H**igh, **S**chool, **B**asque   **2.** Her address is 245 Linx Lane, Espanola, New Mexico  87532.    **3. A.** had broken   **B.** shall have spoken or will have spoken    **4.** Five (spaniels), small (spaniels), shaggy (spaniels), the (countryside), green (countryside), Irish (countryside)   **5. A.** ✓   **B.** __   **C.** ✓    **6.** AMV/RA:  Although Macadamia nuts are native to Australia, they are also found in Hawaii.   Macadamia nuts, though native to Australia, are also found in Hawaii.

**Day 103:**    **1. S**tephen, **F**oster, **M**y, **O**ld, **K**entucky, **H**ome, **B**ardstown, **K**entucky

**2.** If you aren't ready, we'll wait – for five minutes. *or* If you aren't ready, we'll wait (for five minutes).    **3.** (Each ~~of the tennis players~~) serves    **4.** A. AMV/RA: rude   B. reign, rein   C. AMV/RA: ally    **5. (b)** lens    **6.** AMV/RA:  Vinnie has never been to Olympia, but he is looking forward to transferring there.   Vinnie has never been to Olympia; however, he is looking forward to transferring there.

**Day 104:**    **1.**  The, Populist, Party, American, Mia    **2.**  After Laura's essay entitled "Famous Women" was read, everyone applauded.    **3.** well    **4.** ~~During the early morning~~, the <u>girls</u> <u>had ridden</u> (D. O. = horses) ~~for two hours~~.    **5.** A. <u>S</u>  B. <u>S</u>  C. <u>C</u>
**6.** AMV/RA:  A hammerhead can refer to a type of shark or to an African bird.

**Day 105:**    **1.**  Did, Lieutenant, Zebulon, Pike, U., S., Army, Spanish, New, Mexico
**2.** "On April 14, 2001, I listened to the President's remarks," said Brian.    **3.** ~~Across the street~~ and ~~past the old mill~~ <u>lives</u> a <u>ranger</u> ~~with his wife and dog~~.    **4.** (a) limb (b) limousine  (c) minister  (d) misery  (e) orator  (f) order    **5.** A. tiresome  B. salvageable  C.  contouring    **6.**  AMV/RA:  All of the campsites were taken; therefore, the camping area by the stream was closed.   The camping area by the stream was closed because all campsites were taken.

**Day 106:**    **1.**  The, Shen, Yang, Zoo, Siberian    **2.**  Read Witter Bynner's poem entitled "A Farmer Remembers Lincoln" if you have time.    **3.** A.  impossible  B. illegal  C.  invalid  D.  uncommon  E.  nontoxic  F.  irresponsible    **4.** A. more carefully  B.  best    **5.** AMV/RA: Jessie fried an egg and ate it.    **6.**  AMV/RA: As the traveler was taking a picture of a Southern plantation, he fell backwards.

**Day 107:**    **1.**  In, Act, Union, Great, Britain, England, Scotland    **2.**  "Our ladies' club gave twenty-one scholarships to seniors," said the president.    **3.** A.  heavier  B. best    **4.** AMV/RA: thesaurus    **5.** A. <u>IC</u>  B. <u>DC</u>    **6.** AMV/RA:  Visiting San Francisco, the family is riding a trolley and sightseeing.    The family is riding a trolley and sightseeing while visiting San Francisco.

**Day 108:**    **1.**  The, U., S., Court, Appeals, United, States, Environmental, Protection, Agency    **2.**  Rule 1:   Pick up paper (.)   Rule 2:   Use trash containers (.)    **3.** We    **4.** concrete/ common    **5. (b)** freighter    **6.** AMV/RA:  The crusie ship that just returned from Mexico docked at Long Beach.   Having just returned from Mexico, the cruise ship docked at Long Beach.

**Day 109:**    **1.**  My, Italian, Floor, Coverings, Unlimited, Fairfield, Avenue    **2.** A. <u>City News</u>  B. "Every Dog Should Own a Man"   C. "The Long Winter"   D. <u>Lassie</u>
**3.** A. (<u>You</u>) <u>Stay</u> ~~in your chair~~.   B. The <u>custodian</u> <u>cleaned</u> the bathroom and <u>vacuumed</u> the hall.   C. Neither <u>Gloria</u> nor <u>Zak</u> <u>may go</u> alone.    **4.** A. <u>F</u>   B.<u>F</u>
C. <u>S</u>    **5.** AMV/RA:  with large polka dots, waking up, dirty and unkempt
 **6.** AMV/RA:  Bobby Orr, a hockey player, is the first defenseman to score one hundred points.

**Day 110:**   1. Did, Dorothea, Lange, **M**idwest, **G**reat, Depression   2. "Will forty-seven books be shipped to Duluth, Minnesota?" asked Kyle.   3. A. <u>F</u>   B. <u>S</u>   C. <u>R-O</u>
4. A. taste(s)   B. will (shall) collect   C. grew   D. painted   5. (c) bland
6. AMV/RA:   James Bowie fought and died at the Alamo in Texas.   James Bowie fought and died at Texas's Alamo.

**Day 111:**   1. She, Crystal, Airport, Route, **M**inneapolis   2. "The class of '92, in fact, had many honor students ," said the commencement speaker.   3. anybody   4. A. hopes   B. lives   C. dashes   D. cysts   E. lice   F. elk   G. mothers-in-law   H. tresses
5. AMV/RA: Janet wants to go to Alaska, but *she won't go alone.*   6. AMV/RA: Anne Richards who became governor of Texas in 1990 was born in Waco, Texas.* Born in Waco, Texas, Anne Richards became governor of Texas in 1990.

*Note:   Should commas be placed before and after a clause such as *who became governor of Texas*? If the clause is important to the meaning of the sentence, do not used commas.

**Day 112:**   1. Mayor, Yazzie, The, Suez, Canal, I, Eastern, Hemisphere   2. Is those kindergarteners' favorite song "Itsy Bitsy Spider"?   3. A. <u>C</u>   B. <u>P</u>   C. <u>C</u>   D. <u>C</u>
E. <u>P</u>   F. <u>C</u>   4. A. Their (opinion)   B. You're   C. Its (fur)   D. doesn't   5. A. healthiest   B. pronounceable   C. evicted   6. AMV/RA:   Jemima wailed loudly when she was stung by a bee.   Having been stung by a bee, Jemima wailed loudly.

**Day 113:**   1. The, Louisiana, Territory, America, Congress   2. "The Star Spangled Banner" is our country's national anthem.   3. infinitive
4.   First and Last Name
     Street Number and Street Name
     Town (City), State     Zip Code
5. (a) beg   6. AMV/RA:   Fog occurs when excess moisture in the air attaches to microscopic dust particles.

**Day 114:**   1. Dino, I, Dunton, Cinnamon, Pass, Colorado's, San, Juan, **M**ountains
2. The <u>Memphis Bell</u> left London, England, at 5:30 in the morning.   3. A. Brenda's son   B. Sheila and Toby's house   C. cats' dish   D. club's treasurer   4. A. There
B. It's   C. too   5. A. reminder   B. sincerely   C. marred   D. tearful
6. AMV/RA:   John Keats, a famous English poet, almost became a surgeon.

**Day 115:**   1. In, Genghis, Kahn, Mongol, Empire, China   2. "Marge, have you," asked Bridgette, "watched <u>Puppet Play</u>?"   3. A. farm's pet   B. tourists' post card
C. Misty's shoes   D. teeth's cavities   4. A. AMV/RA: A locust is an insect.   B. AMV/RA: Go on without me.   5. (a) trivial   6. AMV/RA:   Sarah Jewett was an American author who wrote about life in New England towns. Sarah Jewett, an American author, wrote about life in New England towns.

**Day 116:**   1. President, **W**illiam, Harrison, Indiana, Territory
2. Granite Concepts Co., Inc.
   120 W. Conrad Ave.
   Betterton, MD  21610

Dear Mr. Carnell:
**3.** laughing    **4.** A. card  B. mother  C. birthday    **5.** A. navies  B. buoys
**6.** AMV/RA:  Dora is a loan officer at Bandix Bank located on Jefferson Street.

**Day 117:**    **1.** **O**n, **N**ew, **Y**ear's, **E**ve, **P**iedmont, **T**echnical, **C**ollege    **2.** Marco Polo,
the great traveler to Asia, lived around 1300 A. D.
**3.**  First and Last Name
    Street Number and Street Name
    Town (City), State    Zip Code

                                                Mr. Charles Glove
                                                12 Amble Road
                                                Broken Arrow, Oklahoma  74011
**4.** A. something written, marked, or engraved in a surface  B. sacred writing or book
C. written or printed copy    **5.** AMV/RA:  The old building is being renovated, and it
will reopen in May.    **6.** AMV/RA:  Our picnic has been canceled due to rain; it has
been rescheduled for next week.

**Day 118:**
**1.** I.  Furniture
        A.  Beds
            1.  Types of beds
            2.  Care of beds
        B.  Chairs
    II.  Belongings
**2.** She asked Mrs. Reed, her social studies teacher, if Zermatt, Switzerland, is at the
base of the Matterhorn.    **3.** clause    **4.** valuable (photographs)    **5. (d)** typhoon
**6.** AMV/RA:  Making a cradle for her friend's new baby, Tessa is measuring a piece of
wood.

**Day 119:**    **1.** A. **N**ew, **H**ampshire, **C**limbing, **G**uide  B. **N**orth, **C**heyenne  C. **P**roud,
**M**y, **B**roken, **H**eart    **2.** A hummingbird approached the flower, but it didn't stay.
**3.** s, sh, ch, x, z    **4.** A. Clay and I  B. me  C. we    **5.** A. S  B. S
**6.** AMV/RA:  Their grandpa, a computer programmer, also volunteers at a health clinic.
Their grandpa is not only a computer programmer, but he also is a volunteer at a health
clinic.

**Day 120:**    **1.** **H**as, **C**orporal, **R**io, **H**orst, **H**otel, **P**rice, **P**arkway    **2.** When the artists'
conference meets here, they'll need tea, coffee, and milk for lunch.    **3.** do, does, did,
has, have, had, may, might, must, should, could, would, shall, can, will, is, am, are, was,
were, be, being, been    **4.** A. ous  B. ness  C. ful  D. ly  E. less  F. er    **5.** A.
properties  B. exchangeable  C. spinning    **6.** AMV/RA:  Lady Jane Grey was the
queen of England for only nine days before she was imprisoned.   After Lady Jane Grey
was the English queen for just nine days, she was imprisoned.

**Day 121:**    **1.** **D**oes, **T**ate, **S**he, **W**alks, **B**eauty, **L**ord, **B**yron    **2.** Cars, trucks, and vans
parked along the long, tree-lined street.    **3.** A. well  B. seldom  C. slowly
**4.** secretary, treasurer    **5. (a)** acrobat    **6.** AMV/RA:  Juan ordered a chicken sandwich

with extra mayonnaise on whole wheat bread.

**Day 122:**    **1. A**, Broken, Arrow, Chapel, Holy, Cross    **2.** The <u>Hapton Express</u> leaves at 4:40 on Monday, June 25.    **3.** A. <u>Yes</u>  B. <u>Yes</u>  C. <u>No</u>  D. <u>No</u>    **4.** A. <u>A</u>  B. <u>A</u>  C. <u>C</u>  D. <u>C</u>  E. <u>C</u>  F. <u>A</u>    **5. (d)** straightforward    **6.** AMV/RA: Chopsticks may refer either to wooden sticks used for eating or to a type of piano tune. Although chopsticks are wooden sticks used for eating, the term may also refer to a type of piano tune.

**Day 123:**    **1.** Did, **Dr.**, **Mrs.**, **Wong**, **Oakville**, **Waterfront**, **Festival**, **Bronte**, **Heritage**, **Water**-front, **Park**, **Sara**    **2.** Joyce Davis, R. N., doesn't work at St. Luke's Hospital in Phoenix, Arizona.    **3.** A. <u>P</u>  B. <u>A</u>   C. <u>A</u>    **4.** author, subject, title    **5.** A. balconies B. replied    C. supplying    **6.** AMV/RA:  A mukluk is an Eskimo boot made either of seal skin or reindeer skin.

**Day 124:**
**1.**
       73354 **Stanley Blvd.**
       East Greenwich, **RI**  02818
       November 2, 20—
Dear **Chuck,**
 **M**y new **Ottenstroer** bike is really neat.  **W**e're going riding soon.
       Your friend,
       Chan

**2.** You have too many <u>t's</u> in <u>litttle</u>, Fran.    **3.** <u>shopper</u> <u>crossed</u>, <u>ambled</u>    **4.** A. their (fault)  B. sneaked  C. affected    **5. (d)** dermatologist    **6.** AMV/RA:  Neither Lenny nor Laura can attend the teachers' conference that will be held in Baltimore, Maryland.

**Day 125:**    **1. Does**, **Diamonds**, **Denims**, **Gala**, **American**, **Cancer**, **Society**    **2.** Your lamp, the one that's very heavy, needs to be shipped in a large, sturdy carton.    **3.** A. any  B. anything    **4.** A. AMV/RA: negative  B. stationary  C. AMV/RA: talented **5.** A. scented  B. believable  C. certainty    **6.** AMV/RA:  Whereas hemlock is an evergreen tree, poisonous hemlock is an herb.

**Day 126:**    **1. Sixth**, **French**, **American**, **Lason**, **Private**, **School**, **Representative**, **Loster** **2.** A secretaries' meeting was held last Tues., April 12<sup>th</sup>, at 10:30 A. M.\*
**3.** First and Last Name
  Street Number and Street Name
  Town (City), State Zip Code
       Mrs. Hope Harmon
       12342 North Lane
       Rusk, Texas   75785
**4.** shaggy, shank, shanty, shapely, shark    **5. (b)** hazardous    **6.** AMV/RA:  This silk shirt may be dry-cleaned, but this rayon one must be dry-cleaned.

\*Note:  Some texts teach that this may appear without periods and/or lower case letters.

**Day 127:**    **1. Have**, **Mario**, **Waterpocket**, **Canyon**, **Utah**    **2.** The building of the

Panama Canal began in 1904; however, it didn't open until 1914.    **3.** is    **4.** ~~At the grand opening of the store~~, the <u>owner</u> <u>gave</u> (D. O. = pens) ~~to his customers~~.    **5.** A. <u>CX</u>  B. <u>C</u>    **6.** AMV/RA:  After Troy had just baked chocolate chip cookies, his brother and sister ate all of them.  Troy's brother and sisters ate all of the chocolate chip cookies that he had just baked.

**Day 128:**    **1.** Last, Mother, French, Fourth, July    **2.** Jack didn't win; his sister did.
**3.** A. driving  B. driven    **4.** A. <u>N</u>  B. <u>A</u>  C. <u>N</u>  D. <u>A</u>    **5.** A. AMV/RA: You may not go unless *you have proper scuba equipment*.   B. AMV/RA:  Before you learn to drive*, you need to learn safety rules*.    **6.** AMV/RA:  The Zuni Indians of New Mexico are known for their pottery, jewelry, and weaving.

**Day 129:**    **1.** On, February, Governor, Ryan, Illinois, Pullman, Historic, Site, Chicago
**2.** The newspaper article entitled "Eat Out" was written by Gina Liss, a food editor.
**3.** A. girls' ball   B. sister's balloons   C. mice's cage    **4.** <u>Has</u> <u>Talley</u> <u>shared</u> her ice cream ~~with her little brother~~?    **5.** A. beginner   B. deterred   C. forgotten
**6.** AMV/RA:  The Cleveland bay is an English horse that has a reddish brown body and a black mane.

**Day 130:**    **1.** On, Inauguration, Day, George, Washington, Bible, Loni    **2.** In the story entitled "The Gift of the Magi," Della's hair is cut and sold.    **3.** interjection
**4.** A. will (shall) be  B. delivered  C. lay  D. had brought    **5.** (a) obvious
**6.** AMV/RA:  Ken measured the beam and cut it into two identical pieces.

**Day 131:**    **1.** My, Pedro, Na, Pali, Coast, Hawaii    **2.** Your belief, without a doubt, was expressed in a clear and concise manner.    **3.** A. most smoothly   B. more confidently
C. most efficiently  **4.** A. atlas  B. nonfiction    **5.** A. scanning   B. preferred
C. braying    **6.** AMV/RA:  William of Normandy arrived with a fleet of ships  and invaded England  in 1066.   Arriving with a fleet of ships, William of Normandy invaded England in 1066.

**Day 132:**    **1.** Is, Sanskrit, India
**2.**   Bradley Corporation, Inc.
222 Dow St.
Las Vegas, NV  87701

Dear Gentlemen:
**3.** A. <u>DC</u>  B. <u>IC</u>    **4.** AMV/RA:  Carlo <u>or</u> Buddy might stay, <u>but</u> we aren't sure.
<u>Both</u> their parents <u>and</u> grandparents drink herbal tea.    **5.** (a) terminate
**6.** AMV/RA:   Steven likes to play ice hockey and field hockey, but he does not like to play football.  Even though Steven likes to play ice hockey and field hockey, he does not like to play football.

**Day 133:**    **1.** She, Going, Home, Mark, Silversmith, Navajo    **2.** A. "The High Road to the Highlands"   B. "The Pacific States Today"   C. <u>Fancy Cars</u>   D. <u>Oklahoma</u>
**3.** A. <u>S</u>  B. <u>R-O</u>   C. <u>S</u>    **4.** A. brought  B. May  C. You're    **5.** (c) chic

**6.** AMV/RA:  Penguins walk awkwardly on dry land, but they swim smoothly.   Even though penquins walk awkwardly on dry land, they swim smoothly.

**Day 134:**    **1.** The, Grand, Canal, Orient, Emperor, Yang, Di    **2.** Shari exclaimed, "Wow! We've done it again, Mother!"    **3.** A.  so  or somewhat  B. not  C.  very D. too  E. rather  F. quite  G. somewhat  or so    **4.** We    **5.** A. <u>DC</u>  B. <u>IC</u> **6.** AMV/RA:  Rob Roy was a Scottish outlaw whose real name was Robert MacGregor.   Robert MacGregor, the Scottish outlaw, was known as Rob Roy.

**Day 135:**    **1.** Did, Aunt, Ali, Urubamba, River, Machu, Picchu    **2.** A. <u>Serenades</u> B. "London Bridges"  C. "Conestoga Wagons"    D. <u>The Red Badge of Courage</u> **3.** A. <u>C</u>  B. <u>A</u>  C. <u>A</u>  D. <u>A</u>  E. <u>C</u>  F. <u>C</u>    **4.** A.  demand(s), demanded, (has, have, had) demanded    B.  swim(s), swam, (has, have, had) swum    C.  fly (flies), flew, (has, have, had) flown    **5.** A. <u>CX</u>  B. <u>C</u>    **6.** AMV/RA:   Tuna, which may also be called tunney, is the largest fish of the mackerel family.*

*See the note on *Day 111* answer key.

**Day 136:**    **1.** Hank, I, Southern, Spirit, Otago, Peninsula, New, Zealand    **2.** "Mr. Lopez's cousin," said Jan, "lives in that three-story house."    **3.** (You) <u>Go</u> ~~into the bathroom~~ and <u>brush</u> your teeth.    **4.** A.  songs  B. cacti   C.  bayberries   D.  calves E.  sisters-in-law   F.  proofs    **5.** A.  AMV/RA: If you have finished eating, *you may leave.* B.  AMV/RA:  Lou is my cousin who *plays polo.*    **6.** AMV/RA:   As Lacy took her little brother's hand and pulled him toward her, she smiled at the same time.

**Day 137:**    **1.** The, Alpine, Garden, Society, Colesboune, Park **2.**

> 3497 S. Rosedale Dr.
> Shelbyville, TN  37160
> Oct. 10, 20--

Dear Monica,
        We've been planning a trip to Toronto, Canada, next ~~summer~~ summer.

> Your college roommate,
> Nanette

**3.** AMV/RA:  to feel, to taste, to look, to smell, to be, to become, to seem, to sound, to grow, to remain, to appear, to stay    **4.** AMV/RA:  He doesn't have any time to do anything.  He hardly (scarcely )has time to do anything.    **5.** A.  marginal    B. politeness    **6.** AMV/RA:   Ricardo's cousin who lives on a cattle ranch in Montana will visit him next week.

**Day 138:**
**1.**    I.  Famous explorers
        **A.** Magellan
        **B** Columbus
            1.   Life
            2.  Voyages
                **A.**  First discovery
                **B.**   Other voyages

**2.** Judith Viorst's poem named "If I Were in Charge of the World" is a short, humorous one.   **3.**   A. **?** interrogative   B. **!** exclamatory   C. **.** declarative   D. **.** imperative
**4.** (a) ladder   (b) lain   (c) lantern   (d) lattice   (e) lime   (f) lint   **5. (d)** weird
**6.** AMV/RA:   Isaac Asimov was a biochemist best known as a science fiction writer. Isaac Asimov, best known as a science fiction writer, was also a biochemist.

**Day 139:**
**1.**
> 1257 West Hearn Road
> Edmund, Oklahoma   73013
> March 10, 20--

Dear Camille,
      Last week my family and I stayed at Hamilton Inn on the way to Luby Bay near Nordham, Idaho.
> Truly yours,
> Jeff

**2.** Because the baby is ill, he is upset, cranky, and crying.   **3.** A. heading   B. salutation (greeting)   C. body   D. closing   E. signature   **4.** One ~~of the flags~~ is ~~on the wrong side of the podium~~.   **5.** A. spanning   B. forgotten   C. warranties
**6.** AMV/RA:   Linen, which was brought to northern Europe by Romans, was the chief cloth of the Middle Ages.   Linen, the chief cloth of the Middle Ages, was brought to northern Europe by Romans.

**Day 140:**   **1.** On, Presidents', Day, Jake, Picacho, Pass, Confederate   **2.** Two-thirds of the three contestants' winnings will go to charity.   **3.** AMV/RA: about, above, across, after, against, along, amid, among, around, at, atop, before, behind, below, beneath, beside, between, beyond, but (meaning except), by, concerning, down, during, except, for, from, in, inside, into, like, near, of, off, on, onto, out, outside, over, past, regarding, since, through, throughout, to, toward, under, underneath, until, upon, with, within, without   **4.** A. prefix = pre   B. root = occupy   C. suffix = ed   **5. (a)** banner   **6.** AMV/RA:   Bobby is limping because he twisted his knee in a fall from his mountain bike.   Having twisted his knee when he fell off his mountain bike, Bobby is limping.

**Day 141:**   **1.** Loren, Did, President, Carter, Oval, Office   **2.** If you're ready for a game, let's play Scrabble, Monopoly, or Rummicub.   **3.** their   **4.** A. AMV/RA: bored, somber   B. AMV/RA: neat   C. site, cite   **5.** AMV/RA:   His brother has asthma.   **6.** AMV/RA:   Ginger is grown for its root which is often dried for medicine or spice.

**Day 142:**   **1.** The, United, States, Senate, Lani   **2.** Chet E. Frampton, Ph. D., teaches part-time at a small, private university.   **3.** I, he, she, we, they, you, it, who
**4.** A. Carrie's friend   B. pencil's cap   C. secretaries' pencils   D. toddlers' rabbit
**5. (b)** chaos   **6.** AMV/RA:   Crusaders who traveled to the Middle East during the Middle Ages brought back perfume and soaps to Europe.

**Day 143:**   **1.** Her, Beth, David, Synagogue, New, York, Alex   **2.** Billie C. Combe, D. V. S., vaccinates our animals and examines them thoroughly.   **3.** A. legibly   B. hard   C. loudly   **4.** me, him, her, you, it, us, them, whom   **5.** A. biographies

B. jolliness   C. shameful   **6.** AMV/RA:   The cashew nut grows at the end of a pear-shaped stalk called a cashew apple.

**Day 144:**   **1.** A. **H**ighlights, **C**hildren   B. **R**ace, **A**gainst, **D**eath   C. **I**mprove, **Y**our, **H**ealth, **C**are   **2.** "The movie entitled <u>Camelot</u> tells of King Arthur's reign," said Casey.   **3.** AMV/RA: antifreeze – a substance that works against freezing
**4.** A. past   B. present   C. future   **5. (b)** consistent   **6.** AMV/RA:   Whereas a man who is knighted is called Sir, a knighted woman is called Dame.


**Day 145:**   **1.** John, Ciardi, **T**ufts, **U**niversity, **U**nited, **S**tates, **A**rmy, **A**ir, **C**orp
**2.** Yes, he, most certainly, will be the lead actor, the star of the play.   **3.** A. <u>A</u> B. <u>P</u>
**4.** family (picnic), fried (chicken), potato (salad), chocolate (cake)   **5.** A. <u>CX</u> B. <u>C</u>
**6.** AMV/RA: Great Bear Lake, the largest lake in Canada, is ice-bound for eight months of the year.

**Day 146:**
**1./2.**

> 77 East Sunnyside Drive
> Scottsdale, **AZ**  85254
> April 1, 20--

Dear **Mrs.** Redford,
      This letter is to let you know that **I** really enjoyed your math class when **I** was in fifth grade. **Mr.** Bencze is having us write a note to a former teacher, and **I** have chosen you. **T**hanks for your help.

> Sincerely yours,
> Bruno Rociola

**3.** A. heading   B. salutation (greeting)   C. body   D. closing   E. signature
**4.** them   **5.** A. distributor   B. organizer   C. protector   **6.** AMV/RA:   Marcy, an architect, is designing an office building.   Marcy is an architect who is designing an office building.

**Day 147:**
**1.**   Slowly, silently, now the moon
      **W**alks the night in her silver shoon;
      **T**his way, and that, she peers, and sees
      **S**ilver fruit upon silver trees.
**2.** Evan's friend, the boy in the blue swimsuit, has won twenty-one medals for swimming and diving events.   **3.** A. AMV/RA: irate   B. AMV/RA: outgoing   C. pane
**4.** hood (with a hood), sleeve (on the left sleeve)   **5. (a)** beg   **6.** AMV/RA:
Making a cup of cocoa, Deka is pouring hot milk into a glass mug.

**Day 148:**   **1.** In, **W**ashington, **D. C.**, **A**rlington, **M**emorial, **B**ridge, **K**orean, **V**eterans', **M**emorial   **2.** She now resides at 1 Watts Avenue, Suite 22A, Goldsboro, NC  27533.
**3.** A. where's   B. I'll   C. they're   D. mustn't   E. don't   F. mightn't   G. I'd   H. we're   I. I've   J. can't   K. it's   L. you'll   **4.** my, mine, his, her, hers, your, yours, its, our, ours, their, theirs, whose   **5.** A. refusal   B. negativity   C. strutted
**6.** AMV/RA:   William Ramsey, a British chemist, discovered argon, neon, krypton.

**Day 149:**   **1.** Is, **A**, **G**arden, **B**ehind, **F**ence, **T**oho, **G**allery, **P**hiladelphia
**2.** Patsy's name has been misspelled on the trophy; however, she'll keep it.
**3.** A. effect   B. regardless   C. Their (reaction)  D. your (kitchen)
**4.**  First and Last Name
      Street Number and Street Name
      Town (City), State    Zip Code
**5.** AMV/RA: Her grandfather is coming today, but *he will be late.*   **6.** AMV/RA:
In proving that lightning is electrical, Ben Franklin used a dangerous kite experiment.

**Day 150:**   **1.** **B**ecky, I, **C**hief, **J**oseph, **S**cenic, **H**ighway, **S**unlight, **B**asin, **M**ontana
**2.** Miss Sabo asked,  "Is this doughnut (one-half gram of fat) on your new diet?"
*or* -- one-half gram of fat --   **3.**   farthing, first, freight, fright, fruit, fry   **4.** she   **5. (c)**
yacht   **6.** AMV/RA:   Lulu became dizzy from the fast ride at an amusement park.

**Day 151:**   **1.** **D**id, **H**omestead, **A**ct, **D**r., **T**opaz, **N**ebraska   **2.** Although my brother-
in-law can't attend the wedding, he's sending a gift.   **3.** A. <u>F</u>   B. <u>S</u>   C. <u>R-O</u> D.
<u>R-O</u>   **4.** A. <u>A</u>   B. <u>L</u>   **5.** A. <u>C</u>   B. <u>S</u>   **6.** AMV/RA:   Quasars which are faint
blue heavenly objects are believed to be the most distant objects in the universe.
Quasars, faint blue heavenly objects, are believed to be the most distant objects in the
universe.

**Day 152:**   **1.** From, **B**., **C**., **J**udas, **M**accabeus, **J**ewish   **2.** At 3:30 in the morning,
the <u>Soaring Eagle</u> landed at Racine, Wisconsin.   **3.** A. <u>I. O.</u>   B. <u>D. O.</u>   C. <u>O. P.</u>
**4.**  First and Last Name
      Street Number and Street Name
      Town (City), State    Zip Code

                       Barrett Company
                       562 Lind Lane
                       Tyler, Texas   75701
**5. (a)** macaroni   **6.** AMV/RA:   Cape Horn, located at the tip of South America, is
known for its strong currents and stormy weather.

**Day 153:**   **1.** **W**as, **B**arry, **G**oldwater, **U**., **S**., **A**rizona, **R**epublican   **2.** No, Mr.
Kartle, we won't need the following:   staples, tape, or paper clips.   **3.** A. May   B.
Can   C. brought  D. swum   **4.** A. AMV/RA: a person who is walking (on foot)
B. a container including earth and growing plants   C. a foot doctor   **5.** AMV/RA:
Logan must take the bus, or *he won't be able to go.*   **6.** AMV/RA:  The whelk, a large
marine animal, feeds on crabs and lobster.

**Day 154:**   **1.**   **C**attle, **I**ndia, **N**orth, **A**merica   **2.** When you write <u>winter</u>, you'll
need to be sure to cross the <u>t</u>.   **3.** A. wiped   B. shall or will remove   C. scrub(s)
D. threw   **4.**   Many (tourists), two (buses), the (area)   **5.** A. coolant
B. classified   C. noticeable   **6.** AMV/RA: Because the freeway traffic suddenly
began to slow, some motorists took the next exit.

**Day 155:**   **1.** **W**hen, **J**apanese, **A**sakusa, **K**annon, **T**emple, **N**ijo, **C**astle   **2.** Two-
thirds of the class watched <u>Where the Red Fern Grows</u> while the others finished their

books.   **3.** A. past   B. future   C. present   D. future   **4.** A. <u>C</u>   B. <u>C</u>   C. <u>P</u>   D. <u>P</u>   **5. (d)** sever   **6.** AMV/RA:   Fiberglass is made when hot, glass threads are forced through a sieve.   Hot, glass threads are forced through a sieve to create fiberglass.

**Day 156:**
**1.**   He lay, yet there he lay,
   Asleep on the moss, his head on his polished cleft, small ebony hooves,
   The child of the doe, the dappled child of the deer.
**2.** A. "Cowboy Sunset"   B. <u>Home Today</u>   C. <u>Motor Boating and Sailing</u>   D. <u>202 Beagles</u>   **3.** Yesterday, n't, rather   **4.** Those (chairs), four (chairs), new (chairs), the (room), living (room), soft (chairs), comfortable (chairs) [Note: Both *soft* and *comfortable* are predicate adjectives.]   **5. (c)** assault   **6.** AMV/RA:  Pago Pago is a seaport located on Tutuila Island, a part of American Samoa.

**Day 157:**   **1.** At, Louvre, Paris, France, I, Venus, Milo, B., C.   **2.** A. col.   B. cm   C. qt.   D. st.   E. corp.   F. mi.   **3.** A. icy, icily   B. dangerous, dangerously   C. kind, kindly   D. intelligent, intelligently   **4.** A. atlas   B. almanac   C. biographical   D. geographical   **5. (b)** chow mein   **6.** AMV/RA:  Tom is nearly finished writing an essay about the French and Indian War.

**Day 158:**   **1.** Are, Lido, Christian, College, Austria   **2.** Although Miller School's committee met on Tuesday, no financial decision was made.   **3.** possessive pronoun = her; antecedent = Chelsea   **4.** A. do/does, did, (has, have, had) done   B. A. believe(s), believed, (has, have, had) believed   C. burst(s), burst, (has, have, had) burst   **5.** A. <u>C</u>   B. <u>CX</u>   **6.** AMV/RA:  After Janie and her family went to the zoo, they went to a fast-food restaurant for lunch.

**Day 159:**   **1.** Was, Peace, Ulbrecht, English, Iroquois, Indians, British   **2.** Your dog, a beagle, is lovable, frisky, and funny.   **3.** A. He is not scheduled for anything.   B. He is scheduled for nothing.   **4.** A. <u>No</u>   B. <u>Yes</u>   C. <u>Yes</u>   D. <u>No</u>   **5.** A. <u>R-O</u>   B. <u>F</u>   **6.** AMV/RA:  Lovage, a plant used for cooking, is native to southern Europe. Native to southern Europe, lovage is a plant used for cooking.

**Day 160:**   **1.** The, Parliament, England, Settlement, Act   **2.** "Wow! You're the first place runner!" exclaimed the coach's assistant.   **3.** operate   **4.** A. AMV/RA: The mother bear stayed near her cubs.   B. AMV/RA: Did his uncle play for the Chicago Cubs?   **5.** A. pressurize   B. cruelty   C. measurable   **6.** AMV/RA: Both the Shetland pony and sheepdog come from the Shetland Islands which are located off northern Scotland.

**Day 161:**   **1.** Thomas, Moran, Mrs., Ving, Western   **2.** "Dr. Killian's neighbor," said Samantha, "is an ex-teacher from Lincoln, Nebraska."   **3.** A. interrogative   B. declarative   C. exclamatory   D. imperative   **4.** A. Either-or, <u>has</u>   B. Both-and, <u>have</u>   **5.** A. hustling   B. crammed   C. enhancement   **6.** AMV/RA:   Babe Ruth who led the Yankees to (win) seven pennants is considered the most famous baseball player in history.

**Day 162:**   **1.** Jay, Has, Grandma, Capon, Springs, Hardy, County, West, Virginia
**2.**

12 Oak Circle
Alabaster, AL  35007
Aug. 18,  20—

Dear Roxanne,
    Thanks for your letter.  My grandparents' house is just two
blocks from yours.  When I arrive,  I'll call you.

Sincerely,
Inga

**3.** A.  heading   B.  salutation (greeting)   C.  body   D.  closing   E.  signature
**4.** A.  May   B.  well   C.  those   **5. (a)** dilate   **6.** AMV/RA:  The Magna Carta
was a document signed by King John of England in 1215.


**Day 163:**

**1.**   I.  **Mid-Atlantic states**
          A.   Geography
          B.   Natural resources
        II.  **New England states**      **2.** The class of 1964 held a reunion at Regal Resort, 22
McRay Blvd., Tulsa, Oklahoma.    **3.** Todd, Ashley, and I    **4.** Within an hour, O.P. =
hour; of the robbery, O.P. = robbery; concerning the event, O.P. = event; in a van, O.P. =
van   **5. (c)** bland    **6.** AMV/RA:  A koala, which is an Australian animal, dwells in
trees and feeds exclusively on eucalyptus leaves and buds.  A koala is an Australian
animal that dwells in trees and feeds exclusively on eucalyptus leaves and buds.


**Day 164:**    **1.** The, Hubble, Space, Telescope, Discovery    **2.** After we've read
How to Eat Fried Worms, we'll write a summary.    **3.** A picnic site and rest area had
been closed during the road construction.    **4.** A.  children's puppy   B.  baby's rattle
C.  cook's hot dogs and buns   D.  teachers' books    **5.** A.  erasure   B.  prettier
C.  raspy    **6.** AMV/RA:  Lucas interviewed for a job selling automobiles, but he was
not hired.


**Day 165:**    **1.** During, World, War, Congress, Eighteenth, Amendment, Constitution
**2.** Mrs. Harrison," asked  Brett, "does your middle name begin with a P?" *or* Mrs. Harrison
asked, "Brett, does your middle name begin with a P?"    **3.** A.  women     B.  businesses
C.  relays   D.  values   E.  agencies   F.  bandages   G.  taxes   H.  moose    **4.** A.  A
B.  P   C.  A   D.  P    **5. (d)** susceptible    **6.** AMV/RA:  The yak, an animal of Tibet, is a
source of milk and meat.


**Day 166:**    **1.** A.  Idaho, Women, Business   B.  Life, Boat   C.  The, United,
States, Its, Neighbors     **2.** His son-in-law, the man in the jacket, is twenty-seven
years old.    **3.** do, does, did, has, have, had, may, might, must, should, could, would,
shall, can, will, is, am, are, was, were, be, being, been    **4.** A.  F   B.  S    **5. (c)**
compliant    **6.**  Preparing a salad, Theo is slicing cucumbers, carrots, and tomatoes.


**Day 167:**    **1.** A, Boston, Phyllis, Wheatly, African-Americn, America    **2.** They
haven't seen Mark, but they'll help you look for him.    **3.** A.  IV   B.  RV   C.  IV   D.

<u>IV</u>   E.   <u>IV</u>   F.   <u>RV</u>     **4.** A. older   B. most reasonable     **5.** A. crabbiness   B. slurred   C. refinement     **6.** AMV/RA:   Although John Jacob Astor arrived in America penniless, he died the richest man in America in 1848.

**Day 168:**     **1.** Governor, Maria, Reno, Democrat, Korean     **2.**   When the class of '91 held a picnic, many couldn't attend.     **3.** collecting magnets     **4.** A. begin(s), began, had begun   B. run(s), ran, had run   C. climb(s), climbed, had climbed   **5.** A. heaviness   B. sparsely     C. immunity     **6.** AMV/RA:   John Chapman who was called Johnny Appleseed sowed apple seeds in Ohio, Indiana, and western Pennsylvania.

**Day 169:**     **1.** The, Freer, Gallery, Smithsonian, Far, East     **2.** The two boys' father had arrived at the <u>Queen Mary</u> at 1:30 P. M.     **3.** AMV/RA: to secure     **4.** A. AMV/RA: We don't want a birthday party.   B. AMV/RA:   Her birthday is in April.     **5. (a)** trivial   **6.** AMV/RA:   Ducks can be divided into three groups:  diving, fish-catching, and surface feeding.

**Day 170:**     **1.** In, Battle, Shiloh, Civil, War, Union, General, Grant     **2.** "A short, snappish dog," said Justin,  "stared at my half-eaten sandwich."     **3.** A. <u>L</u>   B. <u>A</u>   C. <u>L</u>   D. <u>A</u>     **4.** A. a cycle with one wheel   B. 4 babies   C. a five-sided shape   D. a marine animal with eight tentacles     **5.** A. invoicing   B. sensible   C. attorneys     **6.** AMV/RA:   Cyrus McCormick, the inventor of the reaper, started installment buying in America.

**Day 171:**     **1.** "The, Morocco, Allison, Moroccan, Sahara     **2.** No, Mr. Jensen, we haven't seen the <u>Spruce Goose</u> in Long Beach, California.     **3.** (You) <u>Go</u> ~~into the bathroom~~ and <u>brush</u> your teeth.     **4.** A. <u>IC</u>   B. <u>DC</u>   C. <u>IC</u>   D. <u>DC</u>     **5. (c)** judge   **6.** AMV/RA:   Mrs. Yassi, a nurse in a doctor's office, takes careful notes while listening to her voice mail messages.

**Day 172:**     **1.** Has, Pan, American, Health, Organization, British, Virgin, Islands   **2.** When you finish knitting Shawn's sweater,  I'll send it for you, Beth.     **3.** A. <u>S</u>   B. <u>S</u>   C. <u>F</u>   D. <u>R-O</u>     **4.** A. well   B. good   C. well     **5. (c)** friend   **6.** AMV/RA: Wyoming's Jackson Hole was named after David Jackson who wintered there in 1828.

**Day 173:**     **1.** Was, President, James, Monroe's, Hester, White, House     **2.** Jina read her essay entitled "Lucy Darragh's Courage" at a D. A. R. (DAR) meeting.   **3.** A. she   B. me   C. us     **4.** A. AMV/RA:  roof, wasp   B. AMV/RA: eternity, mirth     **5.** A. arrival   B. hoisted   C. alloys     **6.** AMV/RA:  As Lynn gently scooped up her puppy, the telephone began to ring.

**Day 174:**     **1.** Did, Henry, Treaty, Windsor, Selskar, Abbey, Ireland     **2.** It's snowing; therefore, we must drive slowly and carefully.     **3.** A. leaf   B. AMV/RA: suggest   C. ascend     **4.** my granddaughter   **5.** A. <u>C</u>   B. <u>S</u>   C. <u>CX</u>   **6.** AMV/RA:  The minuet, a French dance, was introduced into Louis XIV's court in 1650.   Introduced into

Louis XIV's court in 1650, the minuet is a French dance.

**Day 175:**
1.
    I. **Types of automobiles**
        **A.** **Modern vehicles**
            1. **Foreign cars**
            2. **Domestic cars**
        **B.** **First discovery**
    II. **Other modes of transport**
2. "Have you, Jacy," asked his mother, "done your chores?"   3. covers, use, crayons, markers, pencils   4. A. more respectfully   B. most respectfully   5. (d) clear   6. AMV/RA:  Governor Hans bought a black velvet dress that Carla's sister designed.

**Day 176:**   1. The, Hampton, Court, Conference, King, James, *Bible*   2. This cake, by the way, doesn't contain eggs, but it does have mayonnaise.   3. We   4. A. I.O.   B. P.N.   C. D.O.   5. A. preciseness   B. stingily   C. quoting   6. AMV/RA: Rococo is a very ornate style of architecture that uses shell, scroll, and leaf designs.   Rococo, a very ornate style of architecture, uses shell, scroll, and leaf designs.

**Day 177:**   1. Did, G., F., Handel, German, Messiah   2. A toad, an amphibian that lives mostly on land, has rough, warty skin.   3. A. want   B. takes   C. know
4. A. AMVRA:  That is a hard shell.   B. AMV/RA:  We clapped our hands hard.
5. (c) lungs   6. AMV/RA:  John Carver was a rich man who hired the ship and bought most of the goods for the Pilgrims' journey.

**Day 178:**   1. Tomorrow, Dad, Lieut., Lee, Rainbow, Realty   2. A. Time for Travel B. "Surprises in the Sea"   C. "Amazing Grace"   D. "Mary Had a Little Lamb"
E. City Tribune   F. Cannon in D   G. "At Woodward's Garden"   H. Junior Miss
I. Symptons   J. "America Style"   3. A. Yes   B. No   C. No   D. Yes   E. No
F. Yes   4. and, but, or   5. (d) menacing   6. AMV/RA:  A retaining wall must be built, or the home might slide down the mountain.   If a retaining wall is not built, the home might slide down the mountain.

**Day 179:**   1. The, Batu, Caves, Kuala, Lampur, Malaysia, Hindu   2. When Bob sailed on the Queen Elizabeth 2 to Europe, he visited 10 Downing Street, London, England.
3. A. AMV/RA: Why are you here?   B. AMV/RA:  Stand here.
4. A. Its (paw)   B. You're   C. seldom   D. their (team)   E. well   F. well
5. A. F   B. F   C. R-O   D. S   6. AMV/RA: James Oglethorpe started the colony of Georgia for poor people and brought thirty families with him to America.   Starting the colony of Georgia for poor people, James Oglethorpe brought thirty families with him to America.

**Day 180:**   1. A. Carmel, Little, Lost, Kitten   B. Catch, Me, If, You, Can   C. Eat, Smart, Run   2. "I believe," exclaimed Mr. Tang, " that the girls' team has won by twenty-two points!"   3. A. has burst   B. should have brought   C. must have

broken   D. <u>are lying</u>   E. <u>Have drunk</u>   **4.** Many (pioneers), brave (pioneers), searing (deserts), icy (mountains), a (life), better (life)   **5. (d)** question
**6.** AMV/RA:  Started in 1653, Harlem was first a Dutch settlement called Nieuw Haarlem.  Harlem, started in 1653 as a Dutch settlement, was called Nieuw Haarlem.